Almost Sex

Almost Sex

9 Signs You Are
About to Go Too Far
(or already have)

Michael DiMarco
with Hayley DiMarco

Revell

a division of Baker Publishing Group
www.RevellBooks.com

Hungry
Planet

© 2009 by Hungry Planet

Published by Revell
a division of Baker Publishing Group
P.O. Box 6287, Grand Rapids, MI 49516-6287
www.revellbooks.com

Printed in the United States of America

Library of Congress Cataloging-in-Publication Data
DiMarco, Michael.
    Almost sex : 9 signs you're about to go too far (or already have) / Michael DiMarco, with Hayley DiMarco.
        p. cm.
    Includes bibliographical references.
    ISBN 978-0-8007-3378-0 (pbk.)
    1. Teenage boys–Religious life. 2. Teenage boys–Conduct of life. 3. Teenage boys–Sexual behavior. 4. Sex–Religious aspects–Christianity. I. DiMarco, Hayley. II. Title.
    BV4541.3.D56 2009
    248.8′32—dc22   2009011553

Published in association with Yates & Yates, LLP, Literary Agents, Orange, California.

Portions of this book have been adapted from material in *Technical Virgin* (Revell, 2006).

Creative direction: Hungry Planet
Interior design: Sarah Lowrey Brammeier

"Almost sex is like saying you're almost obese, almost guilty, or almost conceited. If you think you're almost, you already are."
~ Michael DiMarco

CONTENTS

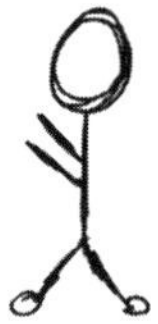

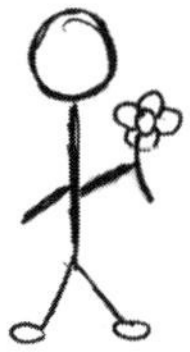

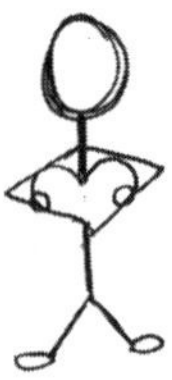

INTRODUCTION

So look at you, holding a book about sex.

Well, not sex but *almost* sex. You could be reading this book for a wide variety of reasons. Maybe one of your parents gave you this book, or maybe your youth group is doing a study. Or maybe you've been crushing on this girl and you just want to know how far is too far so you don't mess things up. It doesn't really matter what your reason is for reading this book; what matters is while you're here, what are you gonna get out of it? And that leads us to my reasons for writing this book.

1. Tons of books on dating and purity have been written for girls (my wife, Hayley, has written some of the best of them!), but hardly any talk to guys alone. It's time to change that.
2. Christian guys need to talk honestly and openly about sex. If we don't, we're more likely to do what we're not talking about. And that's, um, sex.
3. I wanted to write a book that I would have read when I was younger, single, and "almost sexual." Because clearly from my intro, I crossed the "almost" line more than a few times. This is a

book that's honest about a hard topic but that's easy and maybe even fun to read.

4. Lastly, most Christian guys who have sex before marriage are good guys who find themselves going too far, then deciding, "Well, at this point I might as well go all the way." I hope you got this book in your hands before that happened to you.

> If you're not honest about where you've been, then it will be really hard to figure out where you are going.

How far have you gone? Have you tested the waters and decided that they are good? Do you believe that abstaining from sex is God's will for your life, so you do anything but full-on sex? *Almost Sex* is for any guy who craves female attention but just doesn't know where to draw the line. You want more, you really do, but the questions are how much more and when? Can "almost sex" and your faith coexist in your life? What's your criteria for purity—virginity till marriage? And what really constitutes virginity?

For the purposes of this book we'll assume that you really want to please God and that your sex life isn't out of control; it's just something you want to know more about from God's perspective. And so know that this isn't a book that will condemn you for what you've done. But it will hold you to a higher standard, a godly standard. And it will ask you to start to think seriously about your sexual experimentation and how far is too far.

But even more importantly than talking about what to do or not to do, this book will attempt to train you to

almost \ adv
very nearly but not exactly or
entirely

Source info: Merriam-Webster's Collegiate Dictionary, 11th ed.
(Springfield, Mass: Merriam-Webster, Inc., 2003), "Almost."

see the signs that trouble's a-brewin'—the things that you do (or that you let happen) that sneak up on you and before you know it, it's sex.

But before we get started, let's do a little personal assessment. It's always best to be honest with yourself when exploring God's purpose for your life. If you aren't honest about where you've been, then it will be really hard to figure out how you got here or where you are going. So ask yourself: How far is too far? Have you drawn some kind of line in the past? Where is that line for you now? Write it down here:

_____

Then the big question is, have you gone over that line, either accidentally or intentionally?

Yes   No

If someone else was drawing the line for you and they knew what your weaknesses are and when you're vulnerable to slip up, where would they draw the line for you to keep you from messing up?

_____

What I hope you get out of this book is a better understanding of yourself and your limits. I want you to form opinions of your own based on what you know about God and his Word. He has expectations of you, and you can fulfill them once you better understand what they are. So before we get started, let's do a little talking to God. Let's all admit to him that we need to know more about him and that we want control over our sex lives.

Sex and the Single Guy: Michael's Story

I had sex before marriage. Before I was saved. And after I was saved.

There, I said it.

Some of you may now be ready to put this book back on the shelf at the bookstore or start rummaging through your stuff for the receipt to get a refund. And that's cool. There are other books out there where the author either tells you how he remained pure or just tells you what not to do without telling you what he did. Here's the deal. You're gonna hear some deets about my life throughout this book, but before you get too far in, you need to understand one thing: you're not going to get judged, at least not by me. I'm not saying you won't feel guilty or convicted about some things you've done; I'm just saying if you want to read a book by someone who did everything right, you're not going to get that here. What you are going to get is me sharing some scars, some regrets, and the rationalizations that good Christian guys make right before going too far the first, second, and thirtieth time. So in this book I offer you nine signs—some obvious, some not so much—that you're about to step in it. There are signs that sex is sneaking up on us that we as guys either ignore or are oblivious to. Consider this a road map for how to avoid the potholes and sinkholes on the journey to a healthy, happy sex life—when it's your time.

Dear God,
I do have sexual thoughts about girls. I want to be loved. I just don't know how far is too far. But I am willing to learn. I want to please you, and I want to remain pure as you ask me to be pure. Please help me to be honest with myself, to see where I have slipped up, and to get back on track. I want to please you, and I know I can do that with your help. I promise to consider all you have to teach me, including the difficult stuff, and to study your Word. I want to be holy as you are holy.
Amen.

Sweet! Now that we are all on the same page, let's take a look at God's Word and the world's ways when it comes to sex and you. Oh, and BTW, I should tell you that my wife Hayley's gonna ride shotgun on this journey. She's written or co-written a ton of best-selling books on relationships, including *B4UD8* (with me) and the girls' version of this book, *Technical Virgin*, just to name a couple. So sometimes we'll both be talking to you, and once in a while we'll just get her take on some stuff from a girl's perspective. Okay, let's go sign spotting!

Sign #1

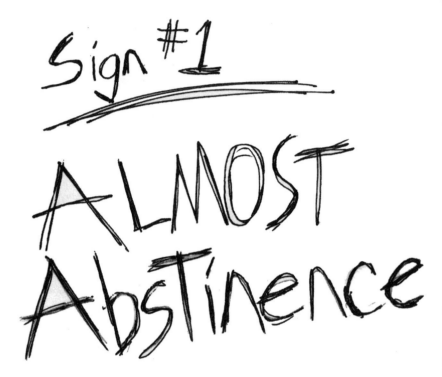

ALMOST Abstinence

You Signed an
Abstinence Pledge That
Doesn't List Specifics

Have you signed an abstinence pledge?

Are you devoted to abstaining from sex until marriage? If so, then right on. Abstinence before marriage is not only God's plan for sex but also the only way to avoid STDs and unwanted pregnancy 100 percent of the time—or is it? Researchers at Yale and Columbia University found that teens pledging virginity until marriage are just as likely to have STDs as their peers. Huh? How can that be? If they're abstinent, what is going on here?

Well, here's the rub (no pun intended). The truth is that those of you who pledge abstinence are more likely to have oral and anal sex than other teens who haven't made the pledge. Shocking? Or not so shocking to you? Guess that depends on your sex life, doesn't it?

There is an epidemic going on today that has to be confronted. Lots of adults are afraid to talk about it because it just seems too freaky, but we're not afraid. If we want to get real with ourselves and our God, we have to get real about our sex lives. We can't keep on lying to ourselves as if that makes everything okay, 'cuz it doesn't.

I pledge
not to do
stuff.
— Mikey

Why are more and more good Christian guys having more and more sexual encounters? And what does God think about "almost sex" anyway? Is he all excited that you found a loophole? Is he happy that those of you who are sexually active without going all the way are having fun and doing what your bodies feel like doing just as long as you avoid the *f* word (fornication)? Oooh, don't get us started. Okay, do get us started! Let's take a logical look at sex and find out where we are going wrong and how to get back on track.

God forbids sexual immorality, or sexual intercourse outside of marriage, as most call it. Right? We can probably all agree on that. (If you're not sure about that, check out 1 Corinthians 6:18: "Flee immorality. Every other sin that a man commits is outside the body, but the immoral man sins against his own body" [NASB].) But then the lines get fuzzy. What is sexual intercourse anyway? Is "outercourse" just as bad, or is it a good "in the meantime" game we can all play till we get married? If you are going to understand your sex life, then you need to understand your position on sex. Yeah, I said it. You need to decide right here and now what sex is and what it isn't and what God allows and

You need to decide right here and now what sex is and what it isn't and what God allows and what he doesn't.

what he doesn't. Then you need to write those specific things in your pledge. And when you think of something that you think should be on there to help you stay pure, add it to your list. We are, of course, assuming that you are a Christian and that you care what God calls sin. You might not have had all the facts in the past, but since you have this book in your hands, it's too late to plead ignorance now.

The wheels are already starting to turn, aren't they? *Have I gone too far? What is too far? Does this mean no more gropey-gropey? Will God forgive me? What will I do from here on out?* Those are all valid questions (though not all are valid words), and none of them are too hard for the power of Scripture to handle. See, if we are all believers here, then we all live by the same code, the same law, the same set of precepts that God set down thousands of years ago and that we can no longer afford to ignore. Check it out:

> Do you not know that the wicked *will not inherit the kingdom of God*? Do not be deceived: Neither *the sexually immoral* nor idolaters nor adulterers nor male prostitutes nor homosexual offenders . . . will inherit the kingdom of God.
>
> 1 Corinthians 6:9–10, emphasis added

We aren't just playing here. This is some serious stuff. If you don't really understand what constitutes sexual immorality, then you run the risk of missing out on your inheritance in the kingdom of God.

We did a little research on the topic, and here is some stuff we found out to help you understand what God defines as sexual immorality, aka fornication. According to Webster's:

sexual immorality: being unchaste

unchaste: guilty of unlawful intercourse

fornication: consensual sexual intercourse between two persons not married to each other

intercourse: physical sexual contact between individuals that involves the genitalia of at least one person

Satan is the master of subtlety. He loves to emphasize the subtle differences between things so that we get confused and start to sin but think we really aren't doing anything wrong. And he's confused us so well in the world of sex. Did you catch that last definition? Let's read it again, this time with *feeling*: ***intercourse: physical sexual contact between individuals that involves the genitalia of at least ONE person.*** See, the enemy of God (he's your enemy too, BTW) has done a masterful thing. He has convinced us that sexual intercourse, which you have pledged to avoid, is penetration and penetration only. The snake hisses that things like mutual masturbation and oral sex aren't included on the sin list God created for you. But guess what? *That's a lie.* If any genitalia are involved, even of just one person, then according to the secular dictionary, you are having intercourse. Surprised?

Let's just get things out into the open. When it comes to your purity, the sexual immorality that God detests includes the following:

Saved by Grace

You probably know more about grace than the average joe, but let us take a small detour into exploring the gift of grace. Understand that if you have been fooling around, hooking up, whatever, without really realizing that God still calls that sin, that doesn't mean you are bound to an eternal life in hell. God's grace, his forgiveness, is there for anyone who wants it and calls on his Son Jesus Christ to get it. If you make a conscious decision today to stop the sex play and repent—i.e., agree to never do it again—you are free from the eternal punishment for those who disobey God.

But with all that said, my brothas, you can't just decide to sin today and ask forgiveness tomorrow without expecting some kind of smackdown. See, God can't let you make a big joke out of his law and then just let you off scot-free. If you are driving through a new part of town and don't know the speed limit, you still are gonna get a ticket if the po-po see you speeding. And God sees everything, yo. You have to get a warning, a ticket, something to change your behavior so you don't do it again, and that means that the consequences of your actions have to be felt. And research seems to show that the consequences of sex are being felt by many a teenager across the world. Sex doesn't get ignored in your heart or soul. It's not something you do that leaves you unaffected. Sex of any kind affects you spiritually, emotionally, mentally, and physically (more on that in "The Great Depression," page 92). So what you think about sex and how you treat it is of utmost importance in your life today.

penetration	petting parties
oral sex	skin on skin
anal sex	groping under clothes
mutual masturbation	groping over clothes

These are all part of sexual immorality. And if we want to get even more technical, then we have to look at verses like Ephesians 5:3: "But among you there must not be even a hint of sexual immorality, or of any kind of impurity, or of greed, because these are improper for God's holy people." God detests not only sexual immorality but also any *hint* of it, so in our definition we can include anything that might make people think that sex happened or is soon to happen—i.e., a hint of it. So let's see, what can we add to the list?

feeling her up

staying the night

her feeling you up

making out in public (everyone assumes you are hav-
     ing sex if you are so intimate with each other)

dry sex, aka dry humping

freaking (on the dance floor)

Yes, simulating sexual acts on the dance floor is a hint (or more). If you disagree, picture a bunch of people in a room freaking with no music playing. Yeah, that's what I thought. Anything that might give a passerby a hint of sexual immorality or—get this—give your body or her body a hint of sexual immorality is a sin. And what about you? Forget the passerby for a minute. When you do anything almost-sexual with a girl, where does your mind go? Do you fantasize about more even though you're not going there yet? Like in a heavy make-out session—ever think about going all the way?

We're not going to tell you yet where to draw the line with the girls in your life. We're not even going to say there is a line, but there is a Spirit. And that Spirit says, "Don't even hint about sex. I won't stand for it." So you have to decide what is hinting and what isn't. And that's why having an abstinence pledge without specifics is a sign that you may be leaving some almost-sex "loopholes" open for the future. After all, you're old enough to make up your own mind, and you're old enough to suffer the consequences of your actions, whatever they may be. But I hope that after reading this and thinking it over, you will have some kind of "come to Jesus meeting" where you really start to think about how relaxed you have let your idea of sex become and stop being embarrassed about getting specific.

In a couple of our other books we used this example, and I think it really helps to think about your time with your girl like this: Pretend there is a cameraman with you, shooting all your moves. Then at the end of the night your entire family is getting together to look at your slide show. "Here I am unbuttoning her top. Here we are rubbing on each other. Here we are swapping saliva." All while Granny and your mom look on in surprise. What would you be comfortable showing the entire fam? If you aren't comfortable doing show-and-tell later that night, then you probably

> Yes, simulating sexual acts on the dance floor is a hint (or more). If you disagree, picture a bunch of people in a room freaking with no music playing. Yeah, that's what I thought.

Almost Abstinence

29

GRANNY

shouldn't be doing it. Consider that the "hint test." You may not be having sex, but using this visualization, Granny will be a good hint detector.

As believers we live by a higher standard than the rest of the world. We believe that our God gave us nothing but truth inside the pages of the Bible, and we trust that if we obey his Word, confess our trip-ups, and create a battle plan to keep it from happening again, things will go well for us. He will shower us with love, mercy, and grace. We trust that if we are obedient even in the hard stuff, he will honor us. It's like his Word says:

> If you *fully obey the* LORD *your God and carefully follow all his commands I give you today, the* LORD *your God will set you high above all the nations* on earth. *All these blessings will come upon you* and accompany you if you obey the LORD your God: You will be blessed in the city and blessed in the country. The fruit of your womb will be blessed, and the crops of your land and the young of your livestock—the calves of your herds and the lambs of your flocks. Your basket and your kneading trough will be blessed. *You will be blessed when you come in and blessed when you go out.* The LORD will grant that the enemies who rise up against you will be defeated before you. They will come at you from one direction but flee from you in seven.
>
> Deuteronomy 28:1–7, emphasis added

Dude, your crops and herds will be kickin'! Seriously, I'm not going all Old MacDonald on you; you've just got to remember that what those verses are talking about are property, your reputation, and your career and calling. God blesses those who obey him. Even though it might seem hard right now, obedience to his Word is priceless. Decide right now if you will serve him or the enemy. Will you be obedient to his call to purity, as wussy as that word sounds, or will you give in to your easy urges and the promptings of the world to satisfy your flesh and the flesh of girls? "It is God's will that you should be sanctified: that you should avoid sexual immorality" (1 Thessalonians 4:3). Will you be obedient to his will? If so, then tell him. Tell him you want massive herds of cows and all that means. Sign your life away today.

> Father,
>   I desire to be obedient in my sexual life. You know when I have strayed mentally and physically, and I ask for and receive your forgiveness right now according to your Word. Today I want to get specific and list everything that I pledge to abstain from to remain pure. I now turn from all hints of sexual immorality and turn toward your Word. Cleanse me from my past mistakes and help me to remain strong in the future. I want massive herds, kickin' crops, and a life that no one can call anything but blessed!
> Signed,

_____

Fooling Around Wears You Out

If you think the hookup, the casual sexual encounter, or being friends with benefits saves your heart from heartache or makes you a power player, think again. You're just a lost little bad boy. You've bought the lie that it's manly to bed every Betty you meet, or at least the hot ones, and you'll settle down when you find "the one" or when you tire out. The problem is, you're just wearing yourself out.

Think of sex as a roller coaster. You keep riding it with different girls; some you really care about, some you couldn't care less about, but you keep riding. And soon the excitement wears off. You know the big climbs, you know where you're gonna get whipped around, and you know how it ends. And it just doesn't give you the thrill it did the first few times you did it. And then when you find that special someone and get married, she's all excited and freaking out because she's always wanted to experience this, well, experience. And here you are all worn out and less impressed than she is.

What you really need to do is stop treating sex like an amusement park ride, and start making the first experi-

ence with your wife a heroic, selfless quest. Instead of "you must be this tall to ride this ride," the carny should only let you on with a ring and a marriage certificate. Don't suffer from almost-sex whiplash by being all worn out. You'll pay a ton for all those individual tickets when God gives you a lifetime pass with marriage! And no long lines either.

Sex Starved

You might think, "That's all well and good, and I get that sex is sin and God doesn't want us to do it outside of marriage, but you don't understand. That's impossible. I have desires. I have urges. And who can go without satisfying them? I mean, it's impossible." We get it. It's hard to resist. It's easy to give in. The feeling makes it easy. Some girls make it easy. Your heart makes it easy. We can tell you from experience that it was the easiest for us to give in when we didn't have a good understanding of God's Word.

In high school I always knew that sex before marriage was wrong. I got that. I wasn't much of a Scripture guy; I was just "moral." I didn't want to be the bad boy; I just wanted to meet a bodacious Betty, get married, and have a bunch of curtain climbers. And I wanted to do it as soon as possible because my parents were both like fifty when I was born, and I vowed I would be young when I got married and had kids so they didn't miss out on stuff like I did with my parents. But because I didn't have a list of "don'ts" or an awareness of what was sex (or even a hint), I would fall hard for girls, think they were the one, and then rationalize, "Oh well, we'll be married soon anyway." You can guess what happened then.

Staying in a relationship because of guilt and trying to make things work is a bad plan. Good plan once you're in a marriage, bad plan for dating.

We had sex. (That was for those of you knuckleheads who couldn't guess.) And the worst part for the girls was that almost every time I'd figure out they weren't for me *after* we had gone too far. And being the twisted "nice" guy that I was, I'd stay in the relationship because of guilt (over the sex) and try to make things work. Bad plan. Good plan once you're in a marriage, bad plan for dating. And this whole dysfunctional forbidden dance all came back to the fact that I didn't know how far was too far until I was like, "Whoa, this is too . . . uh, never mind!" and we had sex. So I know firsthand that the "almost abstinence" plan doesn't work. You need to be honest, exhaustive, and specific on what you're abstaining from.

So don't think that I don't understand your situation, 'cuz I do. And don't think that I'm trying to make it sound easier than it is, 'cuz I know it isn't easy. But trust me, when you fully commit to God's Word and believe it to be true, you get stronger. The pull of sexual fulfillment suddenly doesn't seem as strong.

God's Word is truly powerful, just like it says. "For the word of God is living and active and sharper than any two-edged sword, and piercing as far as the division of soul and spirit, of both joints and marrow, and able to judge the thoughts and intentions of the heart" (Hebrews 4:12). It isn't some weak formula for having a better life; it is power. It is ultimate truth, and it is life-changing. So don't worry about how you're going to stop or how you're going to control yourself. You just are. Trust us. God and his Word are going to help you.

What we want to give you in the following pages is more ammo—more ways to cool down and take back control of your life. We want to make you aware of things you are doing that might be leading you into danger. Once you start to understand where your boundaries are, you will gain strength to stay pure.

Sign #2

Professional Wrestler

You're a Physical Flirt
with the Opposite Sex

I had a couple of buddies who wrestled in high school and college,

and they were always cutting weight. You know, dressing in warm clothes, spitting into cups (sometimes with chew), trying to lose water weight to make their weight class for their upcoming match. That's one of the reasons I never wrestled. It just seemed insane. That, and I loved donuts. The other reason was that they were relentlessly mocked for rolling around on a mat grappling with another guy. It wasn't until I saw wrestling with folding chairs and metal garbage cans getting smashed over people's heads that I came to understand the beauty of wrestling! (I kid.) So now that we've got cringe-worthy pictures of singlet-wearing guys rolling around the floor together in our minds, let's wrestle a bit with some more subtle moments of guy-on-girl action.

The guy who's looking to be a good guy but still have a little fun with a little innocent physical flirting is laying the foundation for sexual foreplay. What might seem like just a fun and safe little encounter could actually be giving you and the girl a mixed message. And

in the end it could lead you to more sexual intimacy than you had planned, especially with those aggressive girls who seem to be multiplying in numbers in recent years. Just playing around can get both your motor and hers running without you even realizing it, and suddenly you've left playful mode and moved into sex-starved guy mode.

Innocent flirting or saucy tease games, those things you do that aren't really sex but can easily lead to sex—that's what we're talking about. How nonsexual to be involved in a major tickle fight and fall to the floor laughing, her on top of you . . . your eyes meet, faces a mere inch away, heaving chests, lungs breathless, and suddenly your lips collide. Innocent romance, right? Maybe not. That's why we're going to call out all of these almost-sex games. Check them out.

The Big Rubdown

It's so wonderful when you give a girl a massage, isn't it? She's been stressed all day, and the touching

67% of surveyed teens who'd had sexual intercourse wished they had waited longer.

Source: "National Campaign to Prevent Teen Pregnancy," (Washington, D.C.: 2003), http://www.teenpregnancy.org/resources/teens/avoid/abstinance/absfacts.asp.

and rubbing just makes her feel so relieved and so loved. You're really an amazing guy to give so much without getting anything in return. And after all, it's just a rubdown, nothing sexual about it. Or is there? It should come as no shock to you but for the average guy, touching is a sexual thing. You feel her curves, you smell her skin, you hear her moan, and suddenly you're thinking about what's underneath those clothes. It is rarely a casual thing for any guy to massage a girl—and if you disagree, then how come we never see you all giving each other back rubs in the locker room? Sick! Because of the major testosterone that runs through the body of any normal, red-blooded guy, you are going to be having some sexual thoughts about the girl you're rubbing down. And suddenly your mind is wandering into all kinds of crazy thoughts.

But who cares, right? I mean, it's not like she's thinking the same thing. Or is she? Most girls aren't quite as sexually charged as guys, but there are a growing number of exceptions which should raise a red flag on the rubdowns. But for most girls a rubdown is just that, a nice massage, and she has no sexual thoughts toward you at all. So don't get yourself all worked up over someone who lets you touch them. It's stupid. But the real problem here is you, not her. Whether she's into you or not, your mind wanders, and you can easily start thinking stuff you know you shouldn't. And that's why so often back rubs are almost foreplay. They relax her and get your mind and body ready for more.

You getting it now? Back rubs are an almost-sexual thing. If you want to maintain your obedience to God's Word and not give a hint of sexual immorality, then stay away from back rubs. It's just a mixed message to your hormones and a first step down a slippery slope. Save yourself and don't go there.

Tickle Fight

Ah, the tickle fight. She giggles; you tickle her more. She squirms; you grab ahold of her. Harmless, non-sexual fun. Right? Or is there more to this as well? Just like the back rub, the tickle fight can get all your juices flowing. Your blood gets pumping. Your hormones start raging. Your bodies start tangling. And you can see the ending coming: You tickle her. She laughs, squirms, screams, and giggles. She falls down. You land on top of her. You both suddenly realize how much you like each other as you gaze into each other's eyes . . . and *bam*! Your lips meet, and it's pure make-out bliss. The start of the perfect relationship.

But what's going through your head at the same time? Just her giggle and that's it? Or the next step—the long kiss, the touch, the roll, the heavy breathing, and on and on. Where do your thoughts go when you start to touch like this?

You might deny that your thoughts ever turn sexual in a tickle fight, but come on, let's be honest. Her body feels so soft. She smells great. She's having fun. You're having fun. Your mind doesn't think about more? Your hormones aren't raging? Tickle fights bring out your sexual appetite. If they don't, then why don't you ever have them with Granny? Oh yeah, her hip replacement. But

> A guy never has tickle fights with his buddies because it's a sexual thing.

still, you get how the tickle fight has that almost-sex vibe, right?

The tickle fight is another dangerous almost-sex game to play if you want to be sex-free, because it's just asking for more. And at the very least, you're just leading yourself on to thinking there might be something more. So be careful.

Nap Time

It's just so cozy. It's a lazy Saturday. Your parents or roommates are out. You're watching an old movie together, and then it hits you. You're both tired, and it's so comfortable being together, so why not take a nap? I mean, it's harmless, right? So you cuddle up in the best position ever, the spoon. In this close position you can feel her heart beat. She's warm all over. Your mouth starts to water. Let's just say that it doesn't take a psychic to figure out where this is going. It's almost sex. Yes, it is. And besides, talk about a "hint" of sexual immorality. When the family walks in, they can think all kinds of things. I mean, you're sharing a bed, sofa, or cozy blanket on the floor—it's a sexual position. Let's just forget about the hint on this one. This goes way beyond a hint because it puts you both horizontal. It paves the way perfectly for sexual intimacy.

If you are taking naps with girls, then you're feeding your raging hormones and hers and making it almost impossible not to go further. Not to sound totally prudish here, but just think about it. Don't lie down together and you can save yourself from falling into the sexual temptation that God's Word warns us against.

Bro Speak
from Michael

Tim from college wrote:

"I'm writing in your response to your comments about how tickle fights are sexual. How can you consider this sexual when tickle fights originate when you're a child? Tickle fights can occur between siblings or parents and their child. Men not tickling each other isn't a reference to the sexual nature of tickle fights but instead an example of societal norms and the homophobic nature of most males. I look forward to your response."

Your logic would also suggest that boys and girls bathing together as toddlers is proof that teens and adults should be able to bathe together without it being sexual. Do you still take baths with your mom? Of course not, because your mom said "at some point this is inappropriate and has sexual connotations." A little thing called puberty happens between being a child and an adult, and that tends to change the context.

As far as societal norms and homophobia, you're right! When I played sports in college, all the guys showered and changed clothes in front of each other, but we certainly didn't get into tickle fights. Why? Because after puberty, it's part of a male/female ritual to gauge physical interest. The only reason guys tickle (in our society) is to initiate physical contact with the opposite sex and see if she reciprocates. Tickle fights are typically sexual because of the intent, and both guys and girls need to know that they're a step up the sexual ladder from holding hands or a quick hug.

So until you change all of Western society (and every other culture we can think of) one tickle fight at a time, we're going to tell the truth, that tickle fights are about initiating physical contact before a sexual relationship exists in an attempt to see if the other reciprocates. Guys that tell girls "oh, it's just a childhood thing" are either lying to themselves or lying to the girl.

Now go tickle all of your fraternity brothers!

Skin on Skin

As you continue to slide down the slippery slope of almost-sexual intimacy, the next thing you are likely to hear from your good friend Harry Hormones is how great it feels to be skin on skin. It's not about sex, just the warm feeling of flesh against flesh. But don't kid yourself: if this isn't foreplay, then what is? And foreplay is for the express purpose of getting our bodies ready for intercourse. It's so totally almost sex. It's impossible for you to lie next to a girl skin on skin and not imagine having sex with her. It's just where your mind goes.

Now, before we go anywhere else on this slippery slope, let me explain one very important spiritual fact. Jesus makes it clear that our sins

Slippery Slope

~~ALMOST~~ TRUTH ABOUT SEX

It is God's will that you should be sanctified: that you should avoid sexual immorality.

1 Thessalonians 4:3

I have written you in my letter not to associate with sexually immoral people.

1 Corinthians 5:9

The acts of the sinful nature are obvious: sexual immorality, impurity and debauchery.

Galatians 5:19

aren't just in our actions but start in our minds. In fact, he's so clear on this that he says in Matthew 5:28 that just thinking about having sex with someone is counted against you just as if you actually had sex with that person. Read it for yourself: "You have heard that it was said, 'Do not commit adultery.' But I tell you that anyone who looks at a woman lustfully has already committed adultery with her in his heart" (Matthew 5:27–28). You can't get around this. This isn't some ancient, out-of-date concept that we gave up on years ago. It's the Word of God written down for all to see and all to be judged by. If you are going to daydream about having sex with a girl, then you've already done it in your mind. And God isn't pleased with sexual sin.

We can't continue to lie to ourselves and say that these kinds of almost-sex games are okay in God's eyes and we aren't doing anything wrong. That might have been the case before you knew the truth, but once the truth is revealed, you have no more excuses. Sex outside of marriage isn't a game to play. It's a dangerous toy that in the end leads you to always heartache, sometimes disease, and often unwanted babies.

Professional Wrestler

The Proverbial Slippery Slope

All of the things listed here are part of that romantic journey down the slippery slope of almost-sex sexuality. The path is obvious, and the slide happens over and over again. If you're on it, you're not the first to go down it, and you won't be the last. Yours isn't some unique trip that is unlike any other; it's run-of-the-mill, happening all over the world, at your school, probably even at

~~Almost~~ Really Good Sex

Sex isn't made for people who aren't married, but sex is perfectly designed for one man and one woman in marriage. Seems to go without saying, but we didn't want you to miss that fact.

your church—and it's terribly, terribly unhealthy for your soul. The progression is usually the same: it starts out with the "innocent" back rub, then goes from there to the tickle fight, to napping, to napping without shirt or pants (after all, it's just like being in your swimsuit), to lying together skin on skin, to heavy petting, to sexual intimacy in any number of ways. All this stuff we've been talking about is made to lead to one ultimate thing—sex. Intercourse, oral sex, masturbation, whatever kind of sex you choose, it's all made to lead there. So the next time you think that what you are doing with a girl is just innocent flirting, tell yourself the truth and get real. It's all almost sex.

Chances are that you probably don't want to disobey God. You want to have a great relationship with him and to be holy and righteous. You love him and talk to him and pray to him, and you didn't mean to fall into temptation. And that's why we've said all this. The more you realize the truth about your own sexuality and put an end to your wrestling career, the more you can control yourself and be obedient to his Word. This is no longer a game; it has ramifications both spiritually and physically, not to mention emotionally. Be safe. Be real. And stop the game. Sex isn't made for that.

Sign #3
_____

MR.

Needy

You Think Sex Is a Need

When it comes to fooling around and sex, guys keep repeating a whole bunch of lies to themselves.

But things you say in order to make you feel less guilty about going too far physically don't relieve the guilt of what you are doing. And one of the biggest signs that you're going to have sex soon, even if you're not having it now, is that you think sex is a need. You know, an "I HAVE NEEDS!" need. If you believe this and you believe God's Word, one of them has to be wrong.

Look, if sex was a need for every guy, then God's Word would outline how that need should be met, right? And the Bible does outline when to have sex—during marriage and not before. So, logically speaking, you must not *need* sex before marriage. You *want* sex before marriage, but you *need* a *wife* to get that want. But even faced with this logic, some guys come up with ideas or excuses for fulfilling their "needs." So for specificity's sake, let's take a look and see if they make sense when you look at them through logic and the Word of God.

Friends with Benefits

A friend with benefits is a girl you hook up with just for the physical but never commit to as a boyfriend (or husband). It seems effortless, a great alternative to a major case of the lonelies. You are friends. You like each other's company. Neither one of you has a significant other. So why not hook up, have some fun, and call it a day? Seems almost healthy. How much more detached and unemotional could you be? With this revolutionary arrangement there isn't any jealousy or hurt feelings. You don't feel trapped in a relationship that isn't "all that." You have a friend and you have the benefits. Bingo! What a great combo. You dive into a "no strings attached" relationship that fills your need to "get a little lovin'" but does it without any of the risk of commitment.

Sounds like power, doesn't it? You're in control of your own destiny, not hurting anybody, because you both agreed it's just for fun. Where's the harm in that? Sounds like a good arrangement as long as you aren't violating your abstinence list, but is it? Let's take a closer look and see what's really going on in FWB.

In biblical days when a man was "lonely" and wanted some action, he would find a girl and fool around with her. Not much has changed in the FWB model, except the name. In Bible days they had another name for a relationship where a guy used a girl to fulfill his sexual "needs." You wanna guess what it was? Here, let us help you:

> Don't lust for her beauty. Don't let her coy glances seduce you. For a prostitute will bring you to poverty, but sleeping with another man's wife will cost you your life.

Can a man scoop a flame into his lap and not have his clothes catch on fire? Can he walk on hot coals and not blister his feet? So it is with the man who sleeps with another man's wife. He who embraces her will not go unpunished.

Proverbs 6:25–29 NLT

Did you catch that? They used to call someone you fooled around with who you weren't married to *a prostitute*. I know, it sounds harsh, but hey, the only difference here is that there's no money exchanging hands. She's still not your wife, but she'll be someone else's wife at some point in the future. And that means she's not yours to fool around with. So hands off. Okay, right now some of you are saying, "She's not a prostitute if we're not having sex; we're just friends making out. It's harmless fun." Check yourself before you wreck yourself, bro. That's total insanity. Are you gonna keep doing that when you get a "real" girlfriend? Why not? Maybe because it means more than the lies you're telling yourself. It's time to get real.

So what happens to the "friendship" when one of you starts crushing on someone for real? It gets kinda weird. When it comes to fooling around, emotions run high, and some changes are bound to happen between the two of you. So what goes on when one of you finds the person of your dreams? What happens to your FWB then? Do you bag the friendship? Do you just stop that crazy sexy stuff you were doing? How do you walk away

Being a "friend with benefits" is like Starbucks deciding to give their coffee away instead of charging and then wondering why they are going broke.

Chick Speak
from Hayley

But wait, there's more to this thing. Both guys and girls who are taking advantage of this FWB thing say it's mutual and that this somehow makes it okay for both of them. Truth is, that just makes it not rape. But what it doesn't change is your thoughts, the things you both think about when you are together. You know as well as we do that your mind goes all kinds of places when you start to fool around, no matter how far you go physically. And girls' minds can go all kinds of places too, not just physically but emotionally. Most girls are romantics at heart, and when the hormones start to rage, it can be really hard not to start feeling the rush of romance. And with that romance comes all kinds of heart trouble. She might say there's nothing to the relationship and it's just for fun, but somewhere in her heart she is probably feeling deeper feelings than you were gaming for. And out of that can come all kinds of heartache. You know how emotional girls can get. You've seen them overreact or read between the lines where there was nothing to read. Most girls bond on a deeper level than guys when they fool around; it just can't be helped, no matter how much they protest. So fool around with a FWB and you run a huge risk of playing Russian roulette with her heart.

from what you already started? The truth is that most of the time the new relationship changes things. Relationships drift apart. Feelings get hurt. Tempers can even flare. It's like they say: you're playing with fire. As a guy you need to be more in control than that and thinking more about the ramifications of what you do. When you use a girl for her body, you are on the path to breaking her heart. Very few FWB relationships end with zero heartache. So think before you lead another person, especially a girl, down the path of self-destruction.

Essentially what you are doing when you create a FWB bond with someone is saying that God's way ain't your way. You've decided that the sexual life that God considers so sacred isn't really a big deal at all. And you are spitting in his face. You are telling God and everyone who knows about your arrangement that your physical needs are of ultimate importance—more important than your faith and more important than God's law. FWB might seem like a simple, uncomplicated relationship, but the truth is that it's one of the most complicated ones you can create. You give away a very special part of yourself, and you take a very special part of her. You lead the mind and the heart of the girl down all kinds of paths. And worst of all, you cheapen the sexual relationship. You make sex or almost sex, all that intimate stuff, disposable. In other words, you practice cheapness. You are creating for yourself and your friend a world where your body and your sexuality are cheap. Hey, it's so cheap it's free. And then when it comes to the marriage you may someday have, look out, because you will have set a precedent for yourself when it comes to sex stuff, and that precedent is that *it's no big deal*. But God says it's a huge deal. It's the thing that you only share with one woman, your wife. It's meant to be a special thing between the two of you, not a need that you have to have quenched however you can. How do married men with that attitude quench that "need"? You remember the word *prostitute*?

Friends with benefits might seem like a simple, uncomplicated relationship. But the truth is that it's one of the most complicated ones you can make.

You also have to consider what your fooling around will do to the heart of the girl who was meant for you. When you get married, all the fooling around you did doesn't just disappear. It stays forever, like a stain on your heart. And it can make all kinds of messes with your future wife. She might have feelings of jealousy over your past. You might compare her to others. Or you might develop really stupid habits that aren't pleasing to her or to God. So before you try to hook up with your FWB, take a minute to think about your future as much as you think about your sex drive.

Face it, FWB is not in your best interest. It establishes in your mind and the minds of those around you that your sexuality is cheap and that your perceived needs take precedence over God and his law. And it opens you up for a world of heartache when the situation changes. If you think you have more control over your love life by having a friend with benefits, you are lying to yourself. You've only cheapened your value in the eyes of your friend and the world.

Mr. Needy

57

Stolen Love

Another fantasy we can live under is the fantasy of stolen love. It's simple and it goes like this. When a girl is dating another guy and she dumps him to be with you, you feel great. You think, "Wow, I have something he doesn't." And so start the lies. Guys are weird that way. We're ultracompetitive. The truth of the matter, though, is that you aren't more of a man. You're just more of what she wants *for now*. Because as we often say: *if I'll do it for you, I'll do it to you*. If a girl will break up with someone to be with you, her character shows that she will break up with you to be with someone else. So don't buy the lie that you are more of a man because she left him to be with you. You are just the guy in her sights for now. It doesn't speak well for her character to be a girl who loves 'em and leaves 'em. So stop the fantasy. She isn't necessarily better for you than for him; she was probably just feeling restless and ready to move on.

When you lie to yourself about a girl's character, you really lose control. You start to let her flaws taint your vision, and you lie to yourself even more. If you want to be in control of your love life, don't date someone who just broke up with a guy to date you. Make her prove herself by taking some time with no boyfriend before she starts up with you. Then you'll be in control. Then you'll be making smart decisions, not stupid ones.

Aggressive Girls

Sometimes girls can be the aggressors, the ones who are sexually "needy" and wanting to go further physically than you might want. So you think to yourself, "Maybe if I give her what she wants, she'll give me what I want. She won't dump me or, worse yet, tell the world I wasn't man enough to do it with her." And so you buy the lie that sex is a need. But that's where guys who date aggressive girls get it wrong. Sexual exploits do not equal manliness. It means you've put God on the back burner and decided that what this girl or some other guys think of you is more important than true manliness.

Chances are, if a girl is sexually aggressive with you, then she's that way with lots of other guys. And that means that going anywhere with her physically is a big risk, not only spiritually but also emotionally and physically. When someone is aggressively pursuing a physical relationship, that's all it is. Period. It's not love. It's not even friendship. It's just all about them meeting their current "need" with whoever is easy enough to comply.

If you're a Christian guy and a girl is pushing you for more physically, then you're with the wrong girl. No question, no need to pray about it. It's not a godly trait in anyone to be pushing God's law away as if it has no relevance to your needs. The best thing to do with the aggressive girl is to just walk away. Don't keep going out with her and hoping she'll stop going after your bod. Things aren't going to get easier with her because her vision is clouded. Yes, she can stop being aggressive, start obeying God's Word, and have a self-controlled relationship. But you're not called to be her sex detox counselor. An older woman needs to walk her through that. Then, after she has lived faithfully and broken the sex habits of her past, *maybe* she

Mr. Needy

> It's not a godly trait in anyone to be pushing God's law away as if it has no relevance to your needs.

could be the one. But let a more mature man of God like a student pastor or your dad, if he is godly, help you make the call.

The Oral Sex Lie

Not too long ago, a survey of fifteen- to nineteen-year-olds conducted by *Seventeen* magazine found that 49 percent of respondents considered oral sex to be "not as big a deal as sexual intercourse." Furthermore, 40 percent of respondents said it did not count as "sex."[1]

All over the world, girls and guys are giving in to their "need" for sexual satisfaction by casually participating in oral sex. If you're a guy who had no clue about this, we're sorry to burst your bubble, but it has to be addressed because something sinister is at work here. This casual acceptance of oral sex as something as mundane as kissing is a bald-faced lie. So if you have joined in on the casual oral sex craze, let's have a serious look at what you've gotten yourself into.

More often than not, oral sex is all about the guy. It's all about pleasing you and does nothing for the girl other than make her a tool that you can use for your sexual satisfaction. And remember that Webster's definition of intercourse as involving "the genitalia of at least one person"? So much for "almost" sex. And if you think that allowing her to perform oral sex on you will make her feel loved, think again. The truth is, it only cheapens her as a girl. In essence she becomes a prostitute, providing sexual pleasure on demand. Sound too harsh? Well, let's just look at the definition of a prostitute:

prostitute: a woman who engages in promiscuous sexual intercourse especially for money

Notice that they add "especially for money," meaning prostitutes aren't *just* girls who do it for money but also girls who do it for free. Having casual oral sex is making the girl a prostitute, plain and simple. And last time we checked, going to a prostitute wasn't such a good thing. In fact, it's the lowest of lows. See what God has to say about the matter:

> That is why your daughters turn to prostitution, and your daughters-in-law commit adultery. But why should I punish them for their prostitution and adultery? For your men are doing the same thing, sinning with whores and shrine prostitutes. O foolish people! You refuse to understand, so you will be destroyed.
>
> Hosea 4:13–14 NLT

I know, we've used the word *prostitute* twice now, and you can't stand it anymore. You just can't hold back and have to scream, "BUT I'M NOT PAYING HER!" Well, chances are you're giving her something. Back rubs? Companionship? The promise of commitment one day?

It was one thing to accept oral sex as a loophole to God's Word before you knew that it was forbidden sexual immorality, but now that you know, you have no excuse. And God's Word makes it pretty clear here, doesn't it? "You will be destroyed" (Hosea 4:14 NLT). Not a pretty picture. But there is hope. You can stop the tide and refuse to let yourself get dragged down into the lie. As a guy, you have to stand up for what is right. You have to take a stand against impurity and not

HPV

Just because you're avoiding penetration doesn't mean you're not giving her a disease.

Human papillomavirus (HPV) is a cancer responsible for 99.7 percent of cervical cancer cases and the deaths of nearly 5,000 women each year.[2] If ingested orally through oral sex, it can be responsible for both head and neck cancer and oral warts.[3]

allow a technicality to lead you and the girl into sin. To lead someone into sin is a dangerous thing, and you will be held responsible for it.

Casual oral sex cheapens sex for everyone involved. For the girl involved, the mental and emotional ramifications are immense, and that's not something that you should take lightly. A real man never takes the heart of a woman and messes around with it like that.

When you have oral sex, your mind subconsciously believes that girls are just playthings, there for your amusement. They aren't to be loved, honored, and cherished. It's a cruel way of looking at the world and not one that glorifies your God.

The truth of the matter is that all of us have the capacity to lie to ourselves about sex and how far we are going. All of us can call our urges "needs" and ignore logic and God's Word. We disregard the fact that if God says he meets all our needs and we're not to have sex until marriage, then sex before marriage must not be a need. As humans we can easily cover up all the stupidity by calling it a guy's prerogative. But the truth is that these sexual excursions—loopholes, if you will, that you create—are really destructive. They not only devalue girls but also teach you that sex is something "just for fun" and not to be kept as a holy thing. Using girls doesn't build your power or prestige among girls or make them want you more. And it is acceptance of full-on sin in your life. The lies you tell yourself about your nontraditional relationship with girls are slowly killing the very core of who you were meant to be and making you nothing more than a sex fiend without character—not to mention what they are doing to your relationship

A real man never takes the heart of a woman and messes around with it like that.

Mr. Needy

63

with God. Consider his Word before you decide "my sexual fantasies are okay," "forgiveness is just around the corner," or "I'm covered by grace."

> If we say that we have fellowship with Him and yet walk in the darkness, we lie and do not practice the truth.
>
> 1 John 1:6 NASB

> The one who says, "I have come to know Him," and does not keep His commandments, is a liar, and the truth is not in him.
>
> 1 John 2:4 NASB

Sexual sin constitutes walking in darkness. It's a blatant statement that God's law isn't important to you, at least not as important as your sexual satisfaction. And according to his Word, if you think you know him but you purposely choose to sin anyway, you are a liar and you don't know him. Ouch! Scary concept. Don't be one of the ones who think they know God but are really only faking it. Purposely walking in sin—knowing it's wrong but doing it anyway—proves that you don't really know God at all. Now, we all occasionally slip up. That's normal. We confess, repent, and receive forgiveness. But don't lump the occasional slipup in with a choice to live a life of sin. They are two different things, and God makes it clear how he feels about the second when he says:

> Many will say to Me on that day, "Lord, Lord, did we not prophesy in Your name, and in Your name cast out demons, and in Your name perform many miracles?" And then I will declare to them, "I never knew you; depart from Me, you who practice lawlessness."
>
> Matthew 7:22–23 NASB

Stop playing with fire. Stop calling sex a need. A life of lawlessness will be much harder to live with than a life of abstinence, trust me. It is worth any degree of self-sacrifice now to have God say to you when you meet face-to-face, "Well done, good and faithful servant" (Matthew 25:23). You have the power to control your mind and your body. With God's Word by your side, you can do anything—or not do anything, as the case may be. The choice is yours. Be sure to choose wisely, because it will affect the rest of your life.

Sign #4

Don Juan
DiMarco

You're Obsessed
with Romance

Okay, here's a chapter for the nice guy and the bad boy.

Let's start with the bad boy. You know girls crave romance. You know that it intoxicates them more than sneaking a Mike's Hard Lemonade. But are you the type of guy that would get a girl drunk or slip a drug into her hot chocolate to get her to like you or worse, get her to go too far physically? Well, if you're a bad boy, you bet your leather jacket you would. That's why you're "bad," right? I think it's pretty obvious why bad boys are bad; I lived almost a decade of on-and-off bad boy behavior. So let's get to the tougher topic, and that's the nice guy.

Nice guys are the group of males most likely to become obsessed with romance. And being obsessed with romance is a clear sign that you're almost having sex. Think that's a stretch? Check it out. When a guy is obsessed with romance, he's either looking to intoxicate the girl he's pursuing or he's looking to get intoxicated himself. And we all know that being intoxicated does not lend itself to the wisest of judgments!

When we're in love with romance, we miss the little things, like "She doesn't share the same faith as me," or "Sure, she slept around with other guys, but I won't fall into that trap." You see, romance is an intensely focused laser of love. You can see it from miles away, it's an impressive display, and it won't even hurt you if it's shined on the palm of your hand. But what happens when romance, er, a laser gets focused on your eyes? What happens to your vision, your ability to see? That's right: you get burned. You get blinded.

Romance is a powerful momentary thing. It's intensely focused light that serves a purpose, but it's not light to live by. It doesn't fill the room to help you see day in and day out. And a guy who doggedly pursues romance is not chasing a particular girl; he's chasing a particular feeling. And when you chase feelings, what (allegedly) feels better than sex? Don't be ruled by feelings—crack that whip and get your feelings under control! In the immortal words of Devo, when a feeling comes along, you must whip it. Okay, not all feelings but a lifestyle in pursuit of feeling a certain way. Meditate on this: if you're constantly trying to fill your life with romance, you're basically doing exactly what a drug addict does. Drug addicts don't keep using because they like sticking a needle in their arm or how much it costs to keep up their habit. They keep doing it because of how it makes them *feel*.

When you become obsessed with romance, not only do you expose your soft underbelly to almost sex, but you nice guys out there also are in danger of becoming the bad boy. Because once you go down the almost-sex road with one, two, or twelve Betties, romance becomes the gate-

Which is more important to you: sex or romance? Either way, both are addictive and can lead you down the wrong road.

way drug to sex. And then romance no longer is the goal; it becomes a manipulation of the target in your crosshairs. And nothing I just wrote sounds anything like love.

The last thing I'll write on the subject of romance is this: if you want to channel romance in your life, be the strong silent type. Be a man who knows how to show affection without going too far. Be a man who guards not only his purity but also the heart of the girl he's pursuing. A man who truly loves a woman doesn't let that woman endanger herself or hurt her reputation. Now let's look at what you can do to avoid the romance addiction.

Fill Your Life with Bromance

Make sure you have buddies in your life to stay busy with who share your views on staying pure and who you can be open and honest with. This also includes guys who will get on your case if you start looking like a cuddly puppy every time you mention her name. A guy who doesn't have accountability is like a fortress with no walls. And a fortress with no walls is just a big house. The other thing that having bros to hang with does is it shows any girl you start to pursue the type of guy you are. It shows that you have a life and that you choose your friends wisely.

Set a Goal That Will Take Effort to Attain

Set a goal so that when you feel a romance void in your life, you have an activity or goal that will take lots

Bro Speak
from Michael

I can tell you from experience as both a former nice guy and former bad boy: being in love with being in love (being obsessed with romance) is a dangerous drug. Many times right after high school, I was *so* in love that I found myself in the middle of a make-out session going for more. One time, still in my nice guy years, I was making out with the girl I was dating, a Christian by the way, and our hands started to travel all over the place. It was getting hotter and hotter, going for under clothes action, and I jumped up and yelped, "I don't usually do this!" And the nice girl that she was, she kind of acted insulted and chirped, "Well, neither do I! What kind of girl do you think I am?" Talk about a curveball. But the romantic in me read between the lines (incorrectly) and said, "Wow, this was really special for her; she thinks I'm special and I ruined it." So I felt romantically obligated to keep going. Twisted, huh? Chalk it up to staring into the romance laser and refusing to be a man and take responsibility for her (and my) purity.

of time and effort to attain. A great example of this is setting your sights on buying a car, learning to play guitar, or saving up for an international trip. You can basically replace the temptation of sexual behavior through romantic obsession with an activity that helps you use that obsession to reach a more satisfying and less sinful goal. Not only does this work to reduce temptation, it makes you a more well-rounded, grounded person much more attractive to a Betty who values depth in a guy that's got his underwear under control.

Go to the Spiritual Gym

You can't get washboard abs or bigger guns without going to the gym. Likewise, you can't become stronger spiritually without working out. Read your Bible, devotionals, or books like this one, and discuss what you're learning with a like-minded friend or a mentor like a youth pastor or a believing dad, brother, or uncle. You only get stronger with repetition. So reading this book once and saying "I got it" won't fly. You've got to put in the time and effort and up your reps when it comes to pumping up your spiritual strength. In the back of this book, check out "Your Spiritual Entourage" and highlight the verses that speak to you where you're at right now. Then copy them down and memorize them. Text them to one of your bros and have him return the favor. The more Scripture you have locked down in your head, the stronger you're gonna be when the heavy stuff hits your chest.

Following these three tips can help develop healthy passions that lead to productive and rewarding goals. When you avoid the Don Juan trap of romance obsession, you also protect against learning to fall in love with love. That means you've just increased your chances of finding that one-in-a-million girl, because you're actually looking for someone with specific qualities instead of someone who just allows you to be romantic. It's like the difference between being in love with religion or being spiritual versus being in love with the One True God.

Sign #5

Self-Service

Your Masturbation
and Porn Habits
Help Keep You "Pure"

Gotta love a chapter like this one, right?

Okay, so, a show of hands: how many of you can talk openly about porn or masturbation with one of your parents? Not many of you, I bet. Or maybe you can but you *really* don't want to. I lead a men's group, and even these grown men acted uncomfortable when I brought up the topic one night. If you think about it, when almost every adult you know is uncomfortable about a topic, where does that let you turn for advice? If nowhere is your answer, good thing you have this book.

Porn Doesn't Keep You Pure

First let's talk about porn. Almost every man I know was exposed to porn (not counting lingerie catalogs) somewhere around middle school age. And almost always for us guys that grew up before the Internet, it was either our dad or a friend's dad that showed us or just left the stuff laying around or tucked underneath the bed. It used to be that men had to walk into a mini-mart or shady adult store and skulk back to their vehicles to avoid being noticed by their friends, family, or co-workers. My, how times have changed. Now I'm one keyword search on Google away from more porn than I ever saw in my teen and college years. And let me tell ya, I saw a bundle.

Think about it: what is the purpose for porn? To make money for others and create lust in you. Plain and simple.

I've talked to a lot of young men and not-so-young men who have confessed to me that they're addicted to porn. That their hard drives are full of it. That they hide flash drives of pics and vids so that their parents or wives won't find it. One young man who had just gotten engaged and was just about to graduate from college told me about his porn addiction and was shocked when I told him, "You're not ready to be married. You're sleeping around now and you're going to sleep around after you're married." Now he was getting defensive. "*I'd never sleep around on Jenny!*" he proclaimed. I calmly opened my Bible and read him what Jesus said in Matthew chapter five, verses 27 and 28:

> You have heard that it was said, "Do not commit adultery." But I tell you that anyone who looks at a woman lustfully has already committed adultery with her in his heart.

I said, "Bro, you've committed adultery with every woman in those videos. How can you marry Jenny when you're not even sure you can stop?" That's the thing with porn; it's like a drug. At first it's just pics in *Maxim* of your favorite TV hottie. Then it's her "Oops, my breast fell out of my top" paparazzi photo. Then it's wanting to watch the leaked sex tape of her and her rocker boyfriend, just out of curiosity. Before you know it, every time you're on the computer in private, you're surfing off to naughty land, watching harder and harder stuff. And here's how porn damages you:

1. **Porn desensitizes you.** This isn't just about wanting harder and harder hardcore porn; this also has to do with arousal. Most women in the porn industry are more altered and enhanced than Jose Canseco. And if huge breasts with tiny waists and collagen-injected lips are all you want to look at, good luck finding your dream girl at church in Sioux Falls, South Dakota (holla to my peeps in SD). Also, it's a given that most guys who watch porn masturbate while watching or after watching, and that desensitizes you as well. While men working in the porn industry seem like they can "go" forever while having sex, the average woman (read: non–porn star) is unable to maintain lubrication, and sex then becomes unpleasurable, painful, and ultimately unsatisfying because the man isn't able to "finish."

2. **Porn makes you lazy.** For the single guy, instead of doing what it takes to find a good woman to marry and have sex with, porn is a way to "compromise" and have sex with images rather than having sex with a real woman and publicly living a lifestyle counter to your faith. Porn lets you be a "bad boy" in secret, as opposed to the "bad boy" who sleeps around and everyone

knows it. This allows you to lead prayer in your Bible study and no one's the wiser. Except God, of course! Not only does porn make you lazy in finding a good woman to marry, but if you're not old enough to marry, it makes you lazy at becoming a real man. Instead of using all that testosterone and drive to become educated, to become successful in the workforce so you can be a provider, and to grow spiritually in the art of self-control, you stay a little boy in a young man's body, a slave to his urges. I believe the number one force keeping guys from growing up into men until their late twenties or early thirties is porn. And get this: porn makes married men lazy too. When married men watch porn, it's usually because the man is too lazy to communicate with his wife about sex, too lazy to grow the mutual respect and intimacy needed for mind-blowingly great marital sex, and too lazy to control his urges when his wife is too tired, too sick, or too whatever.

3. **Porn is adultery.** Yeah, I said this earlier, but this is a list of reasons why porn damages you, and God *hates* adultery. There's nothing about adultery that "keeps you pure." Sure, you might not be sleeping with your girlfriend, and that's how you've justified porn as your necessary evil. But try that explanation when you're driving a hundred miles an hour and you get pulled over. "Officer, yes, I was going a hundred, but at least I wasn't driving in the wrong lane!" Yes, driving in the wrong lane endangers lives instantly, but eventually someone driving a hundred miles an

hour is going to hurt himself and others. Otherwise, why would it be against the law? And adultery is against God's law.

When you watch porn, it puts you in danger because it distances you from God and creates a secret sin in your life that can damage your relationship with your future wife as well. And just like getting caught by the police, you do have to make an appearance in God's court and give an accounting for what you've done. Calling porn "almost sex" is a technicality at best. Make no mistake, porn is sex for the people that are in it *and for you* if you're viewing it. And that's the opposite of staying pure.

The M Word

Now to the topic that's incredibly hands-on. That's right, the M word. Tons of books and articles quote the saying that 98 percent of men admit to masturbation, and the other 2 percent are lying. The fact is that many young Christian men cling to masturbation as their purity release valve; without masturbation they would ultimately slip up with their girlfriend, and they're both trying to stay pure. But here's the problem: remember what Jesus said in Matthew 5:27–28? If you even think about a woman in a sexual way, that's adultery. So is it possible to masturbate without thinking about any woman, sex act, or body part? In theory, maybe— once or twice perhaps—but I majorly doubt it could be done on a consistent basis. And as we've established already, thinking about a woman in a sexual way is adultery, and masturbation adds your own personal

"Sexting"

Did you know that if a girl under 18 sends you a photo of herself naked, you having it on your phone or computer actually violates child pornography laws? That's right, even if you didn't ask for it, when a girl texts you a top-less photo (a.k.a. "sexting"), you end up facing jail time and having to register as a sex offender.

One in five teen girls (22%)—and 11% of teen girls ages 13-16 years old—say they have electronically sent, or posted online, nude, or semi-nude images of themselves. And almost one in five teen boys (18%) say they have sent or posted nude/semi-nude images of themselves.

Source: "The National Campaign to Prevent Teen and Unplanned Pregnancy Sex & Tech Survey," http://www.thenationalcampaign.org/sextech.

and physical twist to your secret thought life. And laziness, just like porn, is a huge factor either causing masturbation or growing out of masturbation. Didn't you pay attention in the porn section? Here it is again but with masturbation replacing porn:

For the single guy, instead of doing what it takes to find a good woman to marry and have sex with, ~~porn~~ masturbation is a way to "compromise" and have sex with images {in your mind} rather than having sex with a real woman and publicly living a lifestyle counter to your faith. ~~Porn~~ Masturbation lets you be a "bad boy" in secret, as opposed to the "bad boy" who sleeps around and everyone knows it. This allows you to lead prayer in your Bible study and no one's the wiser. Except God, of course! Not only does ~~porn~~ masturbation make you lazy in finding a good woman to marry, but if you're not old enough to marry, it makes you lazy at becoming a real man. Instead of using all that testosterone and drive to become educated, to become successful in the work-force so you can be a provider, and to grow spiritually in the art of self-control, you stay a little boy in a young man's body, a slave to his urges. I believe the number one force keeping guys from growing up into men until their late twenties or early thirties is ~~porn~~ masturbation. And get this: ~~porn~~ masturbation makes married men lazy too. When married men ~~watch porn~~ masturbate, it's usually because the man is too lazy to communicate with his wife about sex, too lazy to grow the mutual respect and intimacy needed for mind-blowingly great marital sex, and too lazy to control his urges when his wife is too tired, too sick, or too whatever.

Now, just like sex, masturbation isn't sinful in and of itself. Married couples can do it in each other's presence or to each other if it's con-sensual. But I've counseled married men whose sex lives are boring and infrequent, and one of the major reasons it got that way was their reliance on masturbation to service themselves at their whim.

Porn and masturbation keep you from grow-ing up and being motivated to find a good woman to marry.

So what have we learned? Besides the coun-ter-cultural, not-to-be-taken-lightly fact that even imagining yourself with a woman is sin, I hope you got the message about laziness, because that's the one aspect about porn viewing and masturbation that gets lost on most guys. Porn and masturbation keep you from growing up and being motivated to find a good woman to marry. And once you're married, those bad habits can keep you from having good communication about sex—or good sex in general! For some spiritual backup on these issues, see "Your Spiritual Entourage" on page 134. The sooner you protect yourself from laziness, desensitization, and habitual sin, the more you can reap the rewards of a holy life.

Self-Service

Sign #6

EMOTIONAL
Slut

You're Giving Too Much
of Yourself Emotionally

If you're a romantic or an oversharer, this chapter is for you.

First you've gotta understand the differences in how guys and girls bond. Most girls bond by talking, while most guys bond by just showing up and doing the same activities. It's like this: girls grade each other on class discussion, while guys just grade on attendance. A guy throws a Super Bowl party. Do his boys show up? A-plus! Now picture a girl inviting a girlfriend over to watch a ball game and never talking about anything personal, just commenting on how bad the ref's call was or how stupid that pizza commercial was. And if you can't picture it, that's because you've never seen such a thing. You're more likely to see the girls talk and get so into personal things that they couldn't even tell you who's winning (or even playing) the game. Girls get closer and closer the more they share their feelings and innermost thoughts. It's just how they are.

So herein lies the danger if you, as a guy, are a romantic. Sure, you want the girl to understand that you're not the average guy and that you "get her." You want her to know everything about you and still love you. It's that age-old desire to be completely accepted for who you are. And how can you be accepted for who you are unless they know who you are? And how will they know you, I mean really know you, if you don't tell them all about yourself? So you talk and you talk and you share and you share. You have long phone conversations that make you feel like she's definitely the one because you can talk for hours. You have conversations far longer than you'd have with any of your buddies, saying things you'd be embarrassed if anyone else heard. You spend eight-hour dates talking and sharing your deepest, darkest feelings. All these things feel like such a fantasyland. I mean, the perfect girl is the one who will really listen to you and like it, right? But what if you're getting more than you bargained for in this arrangement?

First of all, let's get one thing clear: girls love being able to do all the things we just outlined. They do it every day with each other. So out of muscle memory, they tend to do it with the guy that they're interested in. But when a guy does it in return, most girls instantly hit the brakes. And that's because the girl doesn't want the guy to out-share her on the emotional front. Picture emotional sharing as

a gas pedal. Girls are used to mashing their foot into the floorboard and feeling perfectly safe about it with their girlfriends because that's just what most girls do. When a girl is with a guy, she really should dial it back to guard her heart, but oftentimes girls just won't control the sharing. They keep their foot on the accelerator. But here's the skinny. When guys do it in return, girls will respond one of two ways:

1. **Too serious, too fast.** Some girls embrace having two feet on the emotional accelerator of the relationship and get too serious, too fast. Without the guy's foot on the brakes, this couple is about to go barreling down relationship road way too fast, at the very least emotionally (sharing too much, expressing feelings they can't possibly feel for each other after such a short time span, etc.).

2. **Mr. Nice Guy becomes Miss Nice Guy.** If the nice guy who bears his soul and emotions to his lady makes the girl uncomfortable or downright scared that no one has control of the speed of the relationship, she starts tapping the brakes. This ultimately plays out in a big role reversal where the guy becomes the emotional over-sharer and the girl becomes distant or stoic or does the "let's just be friends" move. Trust me, there's nothing worse than being called "one of the girls" because you've made girl speak your primary way of communicating around the (previously) opposite sex.

So why do you think I'm going to say that emotional oversharing potentially leads to sex? For the dude that said, "because you make yourself too emotionally vulnerable," *ding ding ding*! Everyone knows it takes longer to stop when you're mashing that accelerator pedal through the floorboard, and you're more likely to total your car if you hit a tree going 50 miles per hour than going 15. Anyone who follows auto racing knows that speed or acceleration has never killed one racecar driver. Rapid *deceleration* kills. And being emotionally vulnerable with a girl is like rocket fuel for our funny car. You know, those racecars with the parachutes that deploy at the end of the quarter mile? The more you tell a girl your deepest secrets and share with her your dreams for the future, the faster the average guy wants to marry those emotions and feelings with the physical. Guys are taught/bred to be strong and guarded, and we tend to lower those guards with a female we're attracted to too fast and too soon. It's like going 200 mph and relying on a tiny chute to slow us down in a heartbeat so that no one gets hurt. And that doesn't even take into account the guy who repeatedly races down different tracks with different girls, all on an emotionally slutty level.

> The more you tell a girl your deepest secrets and share with her your dreams for the future, the faster the average guy wants to marry those emotions and feelings with the physical.

Emotional Slut

89

Besides the almost-sex potential, the guy who is emotionally slutty doesn't value his heart. He basically gives it away on the first serious date or conversation. And even if the guy who does this repeatedly doesn't get devastated every time, he's certainly not learning how to become a man who provides safety and security for

a woman by letting her know he can control the speed of the relationship. Did you know that on most older trains, a man worked on the train with the sole job of manning the brakes? He was called the brakeman (go figure). Every relationship needs someone who controls the speed of where things are going, and a chivalrous man allows the girl to just worry about the accelerator while she feels safe knowing the man isn't going to let things go too fast or too far.

In the meantime, you can't dismiss the value of your heart, and the Bible speaks to your responsibility to protect it. Check it:

> The one who guards his mouth preserves his life; the one who opens wide his lips comes to ruin.
>
> Proverbs 13:3 NASB

> Above all else, guard your heart, for it is the wellspring of life.
>
> Proverbs 4:23

Protect your heart—and ultimately her heart—by not letting too much out of your mouth. It's not just common sense; it's God-sense. If you give her too much info, she's either going to fall too far too fast, or she's going to lose interest because *she* wants to be the one who falls and she wants you to catch her, not the other way around. So play it cool and be the brakeman. Be careful not to share too much intimacy—emotional or physical—with someone you might not be with tomorrow.

Sign #7

The
GREAT
Depression

You Think Sex Will
Make You Happier

Have you been feeling depressed lately?

Really want a girlfriend but no one is to be found? Or maybe you've found a girl but you aren't sure where you stand with her. Girls can rock your world. They can also make you feel like you've been hit over the head with a rock. Repeatedly. But did you know that they literally can make you depressed? That's right: "One study of 8,200 adolescents, ages 12–17, found that those involved in romantic relationships had significantly higher levels of depression than those *not* involved in romantic relationships."[1]

And while we're piling on about relationships, did you know that suicide is the third-leading cause of death for teenagers?[2] In fact, "one-third of the adolescent population has thought of killing themselves."[3]

The truth is that most of the depression that leads to these bad thoughts comes from relationships. Who would have thunk it? But statistics are proving that if you are in a romantic relationship, you are more likely to be depressed than those who aren't in one. Always thought it was depressing *not* to have a girl? Truth is, it's more depressing *to* have one. Go figure.

Sexual Healing?

It's like this. You might think that you'd feel so much better if you only had a girl and some good, good lovin'. You might think that the sexual stuff you are doing right now isn't the cause of any grief or depression but is instead your hope. But let's take a closer look at that. Is sexual fun really the answer to your blues, or could it be the cause? According to Dr. Meg Meeker, "One of the major causes of depression is sex. . . . Teenage sexual activity routinely leads to emotional turmoil and psychological distress."[4]

Have you ever heard that before? Did you know it has been documented that being sexually active before marriage gets you depressed? It seems like the opposite should be true—"sexual healing," as the old song goes. But the truth is that something inside of you knows beyond a shadow of a doubt that sex outside of marriage is a compromise. A part of you that you might try to keep hidden still says, "This is wrong." That might sound ridiculous to you. You say you love the sex stuff. It makes you feel high. It's all you think about. But let us ask you: Ever feel depressed? Do you just want to lock yourself in your room and shut out the world while you wallow in darkness?

There are all kinds of things in the dating world that can send you into the dark abyss. Let's have a look at a few things that happen to your mental state when you start fooling around with girls.

The Great Depression

95

"Almost Algebra"

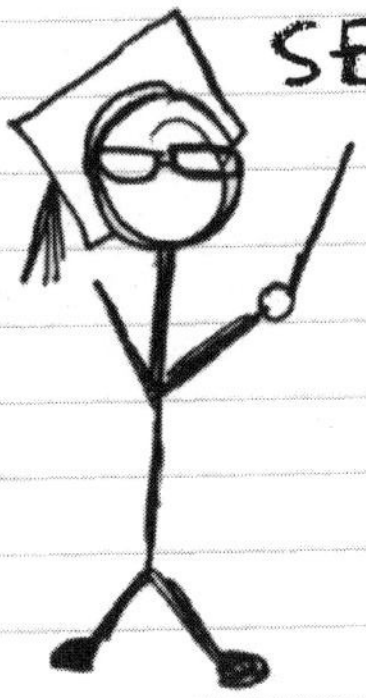

SEX + B4(MARRIAGE)
= DEPRESSION

The Big Breakup

The truth is that if you are in high school, the relationship you are in right now, statistically speaking, will not last. It's a temporary thing. You won't date forever. That means you have two options with this girl. You are either going to marry her or break up with her. Not hearing wedding bells in your near future? Then you're looking at some heartache, either of your own or of hers. Either way, it's going to add some major drama to your life.

And breakups between you and a Betty after you've flirted with or crossed the "almost-sex" line can be brutal on a guy (and the girl, for that matter). One of the most popular ways for guys to deal with breaking up is doing whatever you can to just forget everything. You hate the whole trauma, so you put a fist through the wall, drive ungodly speeds down a dark highway, or turn to something like alcohol to just block it all out. Ah, the joys of premarital sex. Don't be fooled. There are consequences for your "almost-sex" behavior. Even if you aren't going all the way, you are still going to face emotional consequences for how far you do go. So beware.

STDs and You

It should be a no-brainer, but lots of guys seem to just block out the whole idea of the physical dangers of fooling around. You've probably heard it said a bazillion times in health class, but if you are hooking up and having "almost" sex (not even

Even if you aren't going all the way, you are still going to face emotional consequences for how far you do go.

The Great Depression

Young and Infected

In the United States, more than 19 million STD infections occur annually. Half of them are contracted by youth ages 15 to 24.

Source: Center for Disease Control Trends in Reportable STDs "General Research" in U.S., 2003.

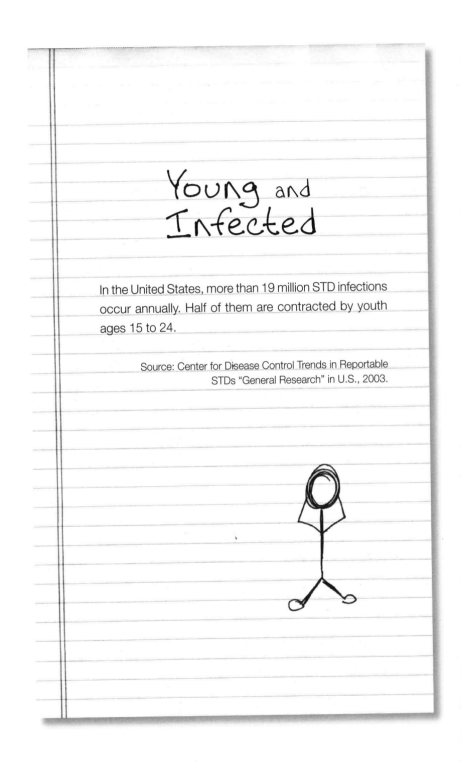

intercourse), you still run a high risk of getting STDs. We're not going to beat a dead horse over this idea. You know it, you get it. Sex games are dangerous for your body. Gross stuff can and does happen.

> One study shows such a strong link between STDs and depression that the authors advised all physicians to screen every teen with an STD for depression.[6]

But did you know that STDs are also linked to depression? Of course, it makes sense. Get a disgusting disease that hurts like heck, and you're gonna feel pretty down. So it goes like this: fool around and get STDs, get STDs and get depressed. Woo-hoo! Good fun. Not! This is seriously gross stuff that even highly educated people like doctors are trying to figure out. "How do we help teens with STDs?" they ask. You'd think it would just be ointments and injections, but the truth is that it goes way beyond that. Now they are starting to screen you for depression if they find out you have an STD. And that's because even the medical community realizes the two go hand-in-hand.

The Great Depression

99

Sex Is Soooo Spiritual

A lot of people talk about sex as a spiritual experience, and it is. It was created by a spiritual God. But imagine (or maybe you are living it right now) what happens when you have given in to that "spiritual experience" and now you are depressed not only emotionally but also spiritually. Deep down you know you've disobeyed your God. You know he was watching and he isn't pleased, so you distance yourself from him. At least you don't have to look him in the eyes and feel the embarrassment of failing. You're literally reliving ancient history, hiding in the bushes with nothing more than a fig leaf, thinking there's no hope. But the truth is, there is hope for you.

If you have done some stuff you aren't proud of and you know God detests, then run away. Run away from the activity and maybe even the girl that tempts you, but don't let the enemy own you by telling you to hide from God. God can and will forgive you instantly. Spiritual depression doesn't have to last for you. You have a relationship with God. You can go to him and get forgiveness. And not only will your spiritual depression lift, but this can be the first step toward lifting your emotional depression.

The truth is that part of you might be bumming over your total loss of control or breaking your commitment to stay pure. And bumming is a process that takes time. Don't expect it to be over in a day. The stages of bumming could be something like this: denial, anger, bargaining, depression, and finally acceptance. But if you get stuck in denial, it will be impossible to get over the depression you might be feeling. Depression isn't something to take lightly. It's a "gift" from the enemy that has to be met head-on and fought. You have to realize that oftentimes it comes from doing something that is inconsistent with what you believe. And then you have to work through your feelings with God and his Word. We don't want this chapter to be a downer. If you are sexually active and depressed, you are already down enough. So let's see if we can't lift you up. God has ways of healing you that outdo everything the world can offer.

Bro Speak
from Michael

It's a sunny day outside and you want to go for a drive. Which would you rather drive right now, one of those pink Barbie Power Wheels jeeps or a real Jeep Wrangler? All but the most twisted of you picked the real Jeep Wrangler. And if you're sixteen or older, congrats, you can legally drive and all will be well with your road/offroad experience.

But guess what, if you aren't legal and you get caught, nothing about driving with the top off and slinging mud will bring you pleasure, only depression. That's because the po-po will call your parents, write you a ticket, and likely delay your future legal driving opportunities. See, my little girl would love to drive my truck, she thinks it would be the greatest thing ever, but the consequences, the potential injuries, would be devastating.

And that's why when we do something that we think is going to bring us pleasure and ignore man's or, more importantly, God's law, we're being shortsighted and childish. Even though you may be confident that you can handle the intense bonding that is sex, you're like a little girl that thinks she can drive; you're ignoring wisdom and what God plainly tells you in his Word.

So before you go driving, make sure you get your license first and you buy the car and don't steal the car. And believe it or not, they've got a permit for sex too. It's called a marriage license!

The first thing to do is to confess. You have to get real with God and tell him what you've done and *own it*. Even though he already knows, confession heals stuff. "If we confess our sins, He is faithful and righteous to forgive us our sins and to cleanse us from all unrighteousness" (1 John 1:9 NASB). And you also need to confess it to somebody else. "Confess your sins to one another, and pray for one another so that you may be healed. The effective prayer of a righteous man can accomplish much" (James 5:16 NASB). Make sure this person is an adult who won't blab about your stuff. Try a youth pastor, parent, or close family friend who will listen and offer you God's forgiveness without condemnation or temptation to gossip.

The next step is repentance, which means you STOP. Stop doing what you've been doing. Turn away. Walk away. Run away. Promise yourself and God that you won't do it ever again.

The depression you are trying to kick will disappear if you do these two things. Sure, the memories will always be with you, but you have to shut them off. Each time you start to remember one of your mess-ups, say, "Yup, I did that," and then stop the memory and replace it with something else. Like God's Word says, "Finally, brethren, whatever is true, whatever is honorable, whatever is right, whatever is pure, whatever is lovely, whatever is of good repute, if there is any excellence and if anything worthy of praise, dwell on these things. The things you have learned and received and heard and seen in me, practice these things, and the God of peace will be with you" (Philippians 4:8–9 NASB). Don't

The depression you are trying to kick will disappear if you do these two things: confess and repent.

Mind Over Matter

Finally, brethren, whatever is **true**, whatever is **honorable**, whatever is **right**, whatever is **pure**, whatever is **lovely**, whatever is of **good repute**, if there is any **excellence** and if anything **worthy of praise**, dwell on these things. The things you have learned and received and heard and seen in me, practice these things, and the God of peace will be with you.

Philippians 4:8-9 NASB,
emphasis added

dwell on what you've already confessed. That just means you don't trust that God has forgiven you and you want to commit the sin all over again by reliving it. Don't go there. Never deny what you did, but always refuse to relive even emotionally what you've already been forgiven for.

Sex before marriage = depression. And getting a girl isn't the answer to all your worries—in fact, she can be the cause of a lot of your worries. Guarding your heart and your body is the best way to avoid depression. But if you've already gone too far, don't fear; God is near. You can have a clean slate and a clean mind. Don't let almost sex or going all the way destroy who you were made to be. Don't let a girl have the chance to hurt you with her words or her body. The guy who's giving in to almost sex isn't as happy as the guy committed to waiting until marriage. Trust the statistics. Believe the doctors and the Big Man Upstairs. Sex games lead to depression, but you have the power to save yourself by walking away now. Trust God to fill that empty space you might fear will be left. He is ready and waiting.

Read over some of God's promises and reintroduce yourself to the truth. You are in good hands.

No temptation has overtaken you but such as is common to man; and God is faithful, who will not allow you to be tempted beyond what you are able, but with the temptation will provide the way of escape also, so that you will be able to endure it.

1 Corinthians 10:13 NASB

Therefore, there is now no condemnation for those who are in Christ Jesus.

Romans 8:1

In him we have redemption through his blood, the forgiveness of sins, in accordance with the riches of God's grace.

Ephesians 1:7

Sign #8

NO
U-TURNS

You've Gone Too Far
So You Think You Might
as Well Keep Going

So what about you?

Have you gone and done it? You've said enough to flirting with the on-ramps and you've fully merged onto the sexual freeway. Have you gone all the way? Feeling good about it, or a little bit guilty? Maybe it was a mistake and you didn't mean to—you just did it. Things got going. Or the pressure was too much. Or you just changed your mind 'cuz it was so great. But whatever the case, it happened. You did the irreversible, and you committed to something that changed your life forever. Having sex for the first time is a life-changing experience. It might not have been what you thought it would be, or maybe it was even better. But what now? What do you do if you wish you'd never done it? Or if you now are starting to realize that it's not the lifestyle you want anymore? How do you change the past? Or better yet, how do you change the future? Lastly, how do I stop asking all these questions?

Putting the You in U-turn

You need to consider a couple things here. First of all, the guilt. If you've given any thought at all to

God's Word, then you have to be feeling a little stupid at best. You are probably asking yourself, "Why now?" "Why did I do it?" And you are probably wondering, "How can God forgive me?" "How can I fix it?" All valid questions. But here's the deal: there are two things you need to do in the aftermath of going too far. One is to trust that when you confess your mess-up to God, he can and will forgive you. And two is to try *not* to be more demanding than God himself. That means don't hold yourself guilty after you've been forgiven. Don't beat yourself up over it, as they say. That means that you agree with God that what you did was not only stupid but sinful, and then you accept his grace on the situation. Practically speaking, that means that you don't go around hating yourself or saying something like, "Oh well, I've already messed up. I might as well keep on doing it since I've gone this far." That's not true—grace isn't a free pass to keep on doing what is wrong. And if you think it is, then you've just rejected the grace you need.

According to the *Tyndale Bible Dictionary*, grace is "the dimension of divine activity that enables God to confront human indifference and rebellion with an inexhaustible capacity to forgive and to bless."[1] This essentially means that God is big enough to get the fact that you are prone to rebellion and that he has the capacity and desire to forgive you for it and, yes, even bless you even though you've done what you've done. To put it bluntly, grace rocks! It's your do-over. It's getting off with a warning instead of a big gnarly speeding ticket. It's something you don't deserve but you get anyway. God wants to forgive you for all the stuff you've done, and he has the power to do so.

See, it's no secret to him when you mess up. It's no secret to him that we all mess up in one way or another. In fact, the apostle Paul writes in Romans 3:23 that we "all have sinned and fall short of the glory of God." So if you are beating yourself up over this, *don't*. It was expected. Humans bad. God good. And that's why he came up with the concept of grace. It's what salvation is all about. Not just salvation from hell and all that hot stuff but salvation from each and every little and big mistake you've made. "For it is by grace you have been saved, through faith—and this not from yourselves, it is the gift of God" (Ephesians 2:8).

It's all about the blood—Christ's blood. He died in order to set you free from yourself. He died so that you could be forgiven and set free from the bondage of sin and all this messed-up stuff. It says so right in Ephesians 1:7: "In him we have redemption through his blood, the forgiveness of sins, in accordance with the riches of God's grace." So believe me when I say you are forgiven. As soon as you confess, you've taken a big leap toward forgiveness. But we'll get to that in a minute. Before we do, I'm going to let Hayley tell you the thirteen lucky words that changed her life forever.

From Hayley

I had thoroughly messed up physically by doing more than I *knew* I should. I finally stopped, but I felt like I was forever branded. Forever bad. I felt like God could never really forgive me. I was haunted by my past and wondered how I could ever get free from it. I remember crying to a friend about my newfound faith. See, once I found out what God's Word had to say, I started to see things in my life that were way off. I had a hunch while I was doing them that they were wrong, but once I started reading the Bible, I knew for sure that I had completely lost it and traveled down the wrong road. I was in anguish. I felt so dirty, so unholy. So *not* grace material. But then someone gave me these thirteen words, and my life was forever changed. This changed everything. Here it is. Read this carefully, and maybe it will help you like it helped me:

"Therefore, there is now no condemnation for those who are in Christ Jesus" (Romans 8:1).

Thanks, babe. Guys, if you haven't read this verse before, or even if you have, you might want to check it out. In fact, go back a bit. Start at Romans 7 and read through this verse. Paul is talking just like us. He's talking about doing all the wrong things and feeling almost compelled to do them. He sees the stupidity of his ways, and then he hits you with a whopper. The most unforgettable passage in Scripture, methinks. No matter what you've done, no matter how bad, or how often, or for how long, there is NO CONDEMNATION for those *who are in Christ*. That's grace, baby! That's amazing (pun intended). It really is amazing grace, how sweet the sound, that saved a wretch like me.

The work is done. "It is finished," as Christ said (John 19:30). All that condemnation was finished the day he hung on that cross some two thousand years ago. So stop the condemnation. You are free. If you've accepted it, it's yours.

Now, we could go on and on about grace. People write entire books on it. So if you are still having a hard time believing it, then do some digging. Look up all the references to it in Scripture. Read a good book on the subject. But most importantly, do all you can to believe it. As impossible as it seems, you can get beyond what you've done.

No Grace for You

Now that we've completed our mini-sermon on grace, we do need to bring up one more thing, and that's the misconception that grace is something cheap. That is, that you can get it today and then go out and get back to the "fun," all the while planning on asking for forgiveness all over again once you've gotten what you wanted. Grace isn't something that can be played around with. It isn't to be taken lightly. After all, it came at a very great price. So if you think that you can accept it while all along planning on going right back into the same sinful situation, think again. God knows your heart, remember? Like Santa Claus, he knows if you've been bad or good, but he also knows if you are planning any more of the bad for sometime in the future. That kind of manipulation doesn't warrant God's grace.

What that means is that if you think, *Oh, it's okay to keep on fooling around because God will always forgive me*, you are wrong. That's taking advantage. And he knows it. It's essentially lying—lying to God that you agree with him about how wrong it was to do what you did. If you are banking on God's forgiveness while deliberately going against his Word, then beware. He can't be fooled.

> Grace isn't something that can be played around with. It isn't to be taken lightly. After all, it came at a very great price.

No U-turns

> The man who says, "I know him," but does not do what he commands is a liar, and the truth is not in him.
>
> 1 John 2:4

> No one who is born of God will continue to sin, because God's seed remains in him; he cannot go on sinning, because he has been born of God.
>
> 1 John 3:9

Seriously? No one keeps *all* his commands. How can you stop sinning? We all continue to sin. It's human na-

"If through a broken heart God can bring His purposes to pass in the world, then thank Him for breaking your heart."

~ Oswald Chambers

ture to mess up. Right? Right, but the person this verse is talking about isn't the average believer who messes up and then repents; this is the person who keeps on sinning because he is counting on the gift of grace. He says stuff like, "Oh, I'll just do this or that, because I can always ask for forgiveness later." Oops! Not according to 1 John 3:9. Now, that doesn't mean that you'll never mess up again. It only means that you won't go on living in sin as if it's an acceptable practice because you are counting on God's forgiveness. In the words of the Soup Nazi (if he were handing out grace in those bowls), "No grace for you!"

> If we claim to have fellowship with him yet walk in the darkness, we lie and do not live by the truth.
>
> 1 John 1:6

Don't become a liar. Once you choose God, you can't choose darkness. The two don't mesh. No taking grace for granted. This is why repentance is so essential. Sure, you might mess up again. In fact, you'll probably mess up again in some area of your life or another, but don't go into the mess-up thinking that it's okay not to fight it because God will forgive you in the end. That's not how it works. It takes a broken spirit and a contrite (humble and convicted) heart to really get to God's grace. You have to mean it when you say, "What I did was wrong."

But here's the amazing thing about how grace works. When going after God's forgiveness, you don't have to ask for it. It's already yours once you've confessed and agreed with God that what you did was wrong. So tell him what you did. Agree that it was stupid, wrong, bad, all that stuff, and then thank him. Thank him for the amazing gifts of forgiveness and grace.

No U-turns

115

Doing the Grace/Repentance Two-Step

So let's review this simple two-step plan to get the kind of forgiveness we have been talking about here. It's all part of God's plan, and here is the rundown of the steps you can take to partake of the grace of God.

1. Fess up. You did it. You know what you did, and you know it's against God's Word. So get real. Get honest and tell yourself and God that what you did was wrong. 'Cuz if you don't, then you are a liar—not our words, God's. Scripture also tells you to confess your sins to another person. Be careful with this one. Don't tell just anyone; make sure he can be trusted. A pastor or trusted friend is your best choice. Having to tell someone you respect what you did can be very embarrassing, and maybe the next time you are tempted to do something wrong, you might remember how awful it is to have to confess it. Check out these words from God's Word:

> If we say that we have no sin, we are deceiving ourselves and the truth is not in us. If we confess our sins, He is faithful and righteous to forgive us our sins and

to cleanse us from all unrighteousness. If we say that we have not sinned, we make Him a liar and His word is not in us.

1 John 1:8–10 NASB

Therefore confess your sins to each other and pray for each other so that you may be healed. The prayer of a righteous man is powerful and effective.

James 5:16

2. Change your ways. The first and hardest step is to admit what you did wrong. But things don't get much easier from there. The next step is to change the way you do things. Stop doing what you did. Give it up. Maybe even give *her* up. Get over it. It's called repentance. And without it, that confession you just made doesn't mean a thing. So here's the deal on repenting:

Repent =
  1: to turn from sin and dedicate oneself to the amendment of one's life
  2: (a) to feel regret or contrition; (b) to change one's mind[2]

And here's what God's Word has to say about it:

Repent, then, and turn to God, so that your sins may be wiped out, that times of refreshing may come from the Lord.

Acts 3:19

Set your minds on things above, not on earthly things.

Colossians 3:2

No U-turns

117

Therefore, if anyone is in Christ, he is a new creation; the old has gone, the new has come!

2 Corinthians 5:17

This all means you just need to realize that what's over is over. Remember, repentance is not only changing your life so it doesn't happen again; repentance also means "to change one's mind." You've moved on. Don't hang on to the past; you are a new creation. Stop worrying about what you did, and turn your mind upward. It's okay to feel regret in repentance. Just give up that old life and move forward to a new one.

No Pain, No Gain

Now, you might have done it all just right. You confessed, you repented, and you changed your life, but the yuck feeling is still there. Don't freak. Don't think you've done something wrong or wonder why God hasn't taken away that feeling of guilt or regret. He can't, or rather won't, do that. His law is good, and it is there for a reason: to protect you. Even from yourself. The things that God forbids can and most often *do* affect you, and not in a good way. That's why he forbids them—for your own protection. And just having confessed and turned from a behavior doesn't take away the effects of your actions. What you did has consequences, side effects. And research seems to show that these side effects are being felt by many a teenager across the world. Sex doesn't go unpunished. It's not something you do that leaves you unaffected. Sex of any kind affects you spiritually, emotionally, mentally, and physically (more on that back in "The Great Depression," page 92). So what you

"Almost Algebra"

YOU + PAIN =
YOU + GAIN

think about sex and how you treat it is of utmost importance in your life today. Forgiveness and grace won't
take away the pain, but they will give you hope and a
fresh start. So don't shake your fist at God if he seems
to be silent while you suffer from heartache, disease,
or your girlfriend's unwanted pregnancy. It's part of the
results of your actions. But rest in the knowledge that
he does work all things together for the good of those
who love him (see Romans 8:28) and that he truly, truly
loves the repentant soul.

To Break Up or Not to Break Up

To break up or not to break up, that is the question.
You've confessed your mess. You've got forgiveness
and you want to move on, so what do you do about the
girl? If you are in a relationship with her, does it mean
you break it all off? Burn all your bridges? Get out while
the getting's good? Not necessarily. That might be your
first instinct. It might be the advice you've gotten from
trusted friends (and good advice at that), but before
you make up your mind, just consider this.

We're not interested in making the decision for you.
We don't know your individual situation. But it's important to realize that once you've gone the distance,
any distance, physically, it's easier and easier to keep
going that far and farther in future relationships. So you
might run from this girl as fast as you can and think,
"Phew! Glad I'm free from that temptation." But the
truth is that the next girl who excites you will be just
as much of a temptation. Usually it isn't about the girl
but about you and your commitment to God's law.
So if it makes sense to you and your situation, you

Teen Marriage

51% of teen marriages end in divorce before the age of 24.

Source: U.S. Bureau of Statistics.

might want to consider talking it out with your girl. If she agrees that you've gone too far, then you can help one another stay pure. You can set rules—places you won't go together or be alone together. Places that are hands-off geographically and physically. You can enlist the help of friends, family, pastors, whoever, to help you keep your commitment to God's law. This could be an important step in learning not to run from mistakes in your relationships but to manage them and repair them. In marriage, if you make a mistake, you can't run from each other; you have to work it out. And dating is the training ground for marriage.

Now, we're not saying categorically, "stay with her." It depends on the individual situation. Some relationships might be really destructive. For example, if she is a nonbeliever, then you *have* to get out. Or if she doesn't agree with your newfound faith in God's law, then no amount of precaution-taking will help you keep your promises to God. So be smart about it. Consider the girl, your God, and yourself, and make a wise decision— one that will best ensure that you will keep your body to yourself.

The End or Just the Beginning?

We've probably said it enough already, but as a kind of period on the end of this "way past almost" sentence, trust that there is hope for you. You can change the way you are living. You can get back to God. You can start fresh. And you can respect yourself again. It probably won't happen in an instant, but then again, you can never underestimate the power of a repentant heart in the hands of an all-powerful God. If you forget how powerful the Father, Son, and Holy Spirit are, just imagine receiving God's grace and forgiveness in that monster truck advertisement voice: "WE'RE FILLING YOUR LIFE WITH GRACE, GRACE, GRACE!" All we can say for sure is that you can become clean. You as an almost-perfect guy can find a fresh start, and you can go on to have a wonderful life with an almost-perfect girl someday. You can have a life that is holy and acceptable and a blast, all at the same time. So spend time in God's Word. Carry it with you. Engrave it on your heart, and hope against all hope that the best is yet to come in your life.

Trust that there is hope for you. You can change the way you are living. You can get back to God. You can start fresh. And you can respect yourself again.

> So we fix our eyes not on what is seen, but on what is unseen. For what is seen is temporary, but what is unseen is eternal.
>
> 2 Corinthians 4:18

No U-turns

Sign #9

Mr. Vague

You Won't Tell Yourself
"How Far Is Too Far"

I hope you didn't skip to the end of the book to read this chapter,

because the entire book was meant to help you answer this one question. This is just the wrap-up, the end of our tirade on sexuality and you. Psych!

If you've read up to here, then hopefully you've already formed some kind of an opinion for yourself on how far is too far. What you need to think about now is how you are going to handle yourself. Seriously. How will you live according to your plans? How will you keep from crossing your line in the sand? A lot of ideas are floating around out there about how to stay pure. There are pledges you sign, jewelry you wear, and commitments you make, and they all are beneficial if, and only if, you have truly decided that you are committed to this new choice. You have to make a conscious decision to change the way you think about sex. You can't walk to the altar to make a pledge just because everyone else is doing it and agree to it because you wanna just give it a shot. Or worse yet, because everybody else is doing it. Never a good reason for anything, BTW. You have to truly make a commitment to yourself—a commitment

Good girls are
looking for
good guys.
And there is
a shortage.
So be that guy.

that saving yourself for marriage really means *saving yourself*. It means giving yourself the best chance at an amazing sex life.

Once you understand your responsibility when it comes to the girls in your life, you're a lot closer to a full understanding of purity and your role not only in your own purity but also in the lives of others. And if you're purposely staying vague on where to draw the line, then congratulations, you're almost having sex. That's because you're leaving all the loopholes wide open for you to stumble through. So you've got to get *specific*. Don't think of it just as a call to purity; think of it as the first step on the road toward true manhood and ultimately finding your almost-perfect girl. Give into your sexual urges at the drop of a hat and you're just putting the almost-perfect girl further and further out of reach.

Figure out who you want to be, what you want to project, and what kind of girl you ultimately want to catch, and then develop your plan for getting there. Godly girls love godly guys. They love a guy who is

willing to step up and be a man and deny his animal instincts in order to protect her and to protect his own relationship with God. The guy who won't fool around is rare, and that makes you alluring to girls who have the same values as you. It makes you different, mysterious—but only if you don't talk about it constantly or make it a huge part of your identity. Because once you make this commitment, you have to make sure not to make it your idol. That means don't brag about your purity. Don't condemn other people's mistakes. And don't use it to "get girls." Your commitment isn't something you use to gain respect or attention. In fact, guys who do that are a real turn-off to most girls. Bragging about how much you can control yourself isn't attractive. Many times girls take that to mean you're not very sexual, and they have an emasculated view of the virgin guy shouting from the rooftops. So just be the guy who doesn't use girls and who hasn't been around the block, not the guy who brags about his faith or his spiritual fortitude.

Those of you who think you've gone too far and now you are feeling guilty—stop. As you confess your sins and accept God's grace, your guilt is replaced with forgiveness. This forgiveness you have because of your relationship with Christ means you are no longer condemned. What you should be feeling is simply conviction, not guilt. You have gone down the wrong path, and your conscience is now tapping on your shoulder, but don't confuse that with guilt. You simply need to tell God what you've done. I know, he knows all, but you still have to tell him and one other trustworthy believer. It's called confession. Then you have to trust that he has forgiven you. And you have to repent—that is, turn away from your old behavior and move toward new behavior. The thing to remember is that if you keep doing what you're doing, you'll keep getting what you've got. And the question has to be, is that enough? Or are you ready to move on to something more?

Now, if you've kept yourself pure and you are now more determined than ever to continue down that path, keep it up! Seriously, you can do it. Good girls are looking for good guys. And there is a shortage. So be that guy. Be the unique one, the good one, who isn't telling everyone how special he is but is showing them how special he is by controlling his hands, his mind, and his body. Decide today how far is too far, and *get specific*. Consider all that you've read and all that God has written on the subject. Who do you want to be? How do you want to be thought of? Take a stand. Hold firm and stay strong through the hard times. You can do it, and you can be victorious.

Drawing the Line

Before you go, try this exercise. Draw the "how far" line right here. If you don't have a line, it becomes a lot harder to stop when you're with the girl of your dreams. So before you put this book away, let's do some line drawing. Below is a list of stuff that you might one day want to do with a girl. They are kind of in a progression from least sexual to most. This is generally the path we take when it comes to getting physical. Have a look.

The double take (this is when you ogle your girl and
   can't stop)
Talking with her
Flirting with her
Touching her arm or leg
Hugs
Holding hands
Touching each other's faces
Arms around each other
Lip kissing
French kissing

And so on. We're not going any further because
there's plenty of space above to start drawing your
line. So have a ponder. Where will you draw the line
when it comes to girls? How far is too far for you? How
far is too far for God? Draw a line under the most that
you want to do with a girl before you are married.
   Did you do it?
   Good. Now you have something to work with. The
next step in keeping it pure is to talk to someone about
your commitment. Maybe a youth pastor, a parent, or
even a really good friend—any believer of the same
gender who will help hold you accountable. Their job
is to ask you, "Did you cross the line?" Remembering
that every time you have a date or spend time with
a girl, your accountability partner is going to ask you
how far you went will really help you when you're
with the girl, because telling your confidant that you
crossed the line is really sickening. The only require-
ment of you is that you have to tell the truth. No commitment of accountability will ever work if you're not

honest with yourself and your accountability partner. So pick someone who won't disown you if you share that you messed up.

Godly girls will think more of a guy who has made up his mind to keep it clean. Once you've decided to go down a dating or courtship road with this "God Girl," talk to her about the line you've drawn so you can be on the same page. That way, if she's not a "God Girl," you can get away while the getting's good instead of her "working on you" to see if she can get you to break your promise to yourself and to God.

Here are some other things and places to avoid if you want to try to keep your line drawn right where it is:

Spending time with her in your room or her room with the door closed

Napping together

Lying down together, period

Hanging out at home alone

Parking to "enjoy the view" or to "just talk"

Body massages

Drinking (you can lose all memory of lines when you do)

Dating non-believers (they won't have the same supernatural source of self-control)

These are just a few situations to avoid if you're going to keep your line where you've drawn it. Having a plan before you get into a relationship will help you handle that relationship the way you want. And writing down that plan helps reinforce it in your mind and heart. So now write it down. Write a small prayer here, including where you're drawing your line and even some of the no-no's above that you're going to avoid. Make it a promise to God. Then, after you've written it, read it out loud to him and sign your name. This is your commitment. Your word. And your word shouldn't be broken. Ask God to help you keep your commitment and remember him every time you get into a sticky situation.

Dear God,

_____

_____

_____

_____

_____

_____

Signed _____

Well, this is it. It's good-bye for now. Hope you found some good stuff in this book. And we pray that your soul is strengthened and ready for the battle ahead. We're proud of you for coming this far. Keep the faith and visit us at **www.ifuse.com** to hang with us and other guys on the same journey.

Michael and Hayley

Because God's
Got Your Back

Confessing Your Stuff

If we confess our sins, he is faithful and just and will forgive us our sins and purify us from all unrighteousness.

1 John 1:9

I have sinned greatly in what I have done. Now, O Lord, I beg you, take away the guilt of your servant. I have done a very foolish thing.

2 Samuel 24:10

Therefore confess your sins to each other and pray for each other so that you may be healed. The prayer of a righteous man is powerful and effective.

James 5:16

He who conceals his sins does not prosper,
    but whoever confesses and renounces them
    finds mercy.

Proverbs 28:13

When I kept silent,
    my bones wasted away
    through my groaning all day long.
For day and night
    your hand was heavy upon me;
    my strength was sapped
    as in the heat of summer.
Then I acknowledged my sin to you
    and did not cover up my iniquity.
I said, "I will confess
    my transgressions to the Lord"—
and you forgave
    the guilt of my sin.

Psalm 32:3–5

Failure

We know that the law is spiritual; but I am unspiritual, sold as a slave to sin. . . . Therefore, there is now no condemnation for those who are in Christ Jesus.

Romans 7:14; 8:1

The LORD works out everything for his own ends— even the wicked for a day of disaster.

Proverbs 16:4

And we know that in all things God works for the good of those who love him, who have been called according to his purpose.

Romans 8:28

Your Spiritual Entourage

137

Getting Back to God

Delight yourself in the LORD
and he will give you the desires of your heart.

Psalm 37:4

Therefore we do not lose heart. Though outwardly we
are wasting away, yet inwardly we are being renewed
day by day.

2 Corinthians 4:16

Now faith is being sure of what we hope for and certain
of what we do not see.

Hebrews 11:1

I tell you the truth, if you have faith as small as a mustard
seed, you can say to this mountain, "Move from here
to there" and it will move. Nothing will be impossible
for you.

Matthew 17:20

But when he asks, he must believe and not doubt, because he who doubts is like a wave of the sea, blown
and tossed by the wind. That man should not think he
will receive anything from the Lord.

James 1:6–7

Strength for Today

Therefore put on the full armor of God, so that when the day of evil comes, you may be able to stand your ground, and after you have done everything, to stand. Stand firm then, with the belt of truth buckled around your waist, with the breastplate of righteousness in place, and with your feet fitted with the readiness that comes from the gospel of peace. In addition to all this, take up the shield of faith, with which you can extinguish all the flaming arrows of the evil one. Take the helmet of salvation and the sword of the Spirit, which is the word of God.

Ephesians 6:13–17

My son, if you accept my words
    and store up my commands within you,
turning your ear to wisdom
    and applying your heart to understanding,
and if you call out for insight
    and cry aloud for understanding,
and if you look for it as for silver
    and search for it as for hidden treasure,
then you will understand the fear of the LORD
    and find the knowledge of God.

Proverbs 2:1–5

So do not fear, for I am with you;
    do not be dismayed, for I am your God.
I will strengthen you and help you;
    I will uphold you with my righteous right hand.

Isaiah 41:10

In you, O Lord, I have taken refuge;
   let me never be put to shame;
   deliver me in your righteousness.
Turn your ear to me,
   come quickly to my rescue;
   be my rock of refuge,
   a strong fortress to save me.

Psalm 31:1–2

What, then, shall we say in response to this? If God is for us, who can be against us? He who did not spare his own Son, but gave him up for us all—how will he not also, along with him, graciously give us all things? Who will bring any charge against those whom God has chosen? It is God who justifies.

Romans 8:31–33

The reason the Son of God appeared was to destroy the devil's work.

1 John 3:8

But Jesus immediately said to them: "Take courage! It is I. Don't be afraid."

Matthew 14:27

God is our refuge and strength, an ever-present help in trouble.

Psalm 46:1

Facing Temptation

Be always on the watch, and pray that you may be able to escape all that is about to happen, and that you may be able to stand before the Son of Man.

Luke 21:36

For our struggle is not against flesh and blood, but against the rulers, against the authorities, against the powers of this dark world and against the spiritual forces of evil in the heavenly realms.

Ephesians 6:12

In the same way, the Spirit helps us in our weakness. We do not know what we ought to pray for, but the Spirit himself intercedes for us with groans that words cannot express.

Romans 8:26

Like a city whose walls are broken down is a man who lacks self-control.

Proverbs 25:28

Breaking Up

Am I now trying to win the approval of men, or of God?
Or am I trying to please men? If I were still trying to
please men, I would not be a servant of Christ.

Galatians 1:10

I remember my affliction and my wandering,
    the bitterness and the gall.
I well remember them,
    and my soul is downcast within me.
Yet this I call to mind
    and therefore I have hope:
Because of the Lord's great love we are not
    consumed,
    for his compassions never fail.
They are new every morning;
    great is your faithfulness.
I say to myself, "The LORD is my portion;
    therefore I will wait for him."

Lamentations 3:19–24

It is to a man's honor to avoid strife,
    but every fool is quick to quarrel.

Proverbs 20:3

Trust in the LORD with all your heart
    and lean not on your own understanding;
in all your ways acknowledge him,
    and he will make your paths straight.

Proverbs 3:5–6

Each one should test his own actions. Then he can take pride in himself, without comparing himself to somebody else, for each one should carry his own load.

Galatians 6:4–5

The suffering won't last forever. It won't be long before this generous God who has great plans for us in Christ—eternal and glorious plans they are!—will have you put together and on your feet for good.

1 Peter 5:10 Message

Pre-Date Preparation

Do not conform any longer to the pattern of this world, but be transformed by the renewing of your mind. Then you will be able to test and approve what God's will is—his good, pleasing and perfect will.

Romans 12:2

The end of all things is near. Therefore be clear minded and self-controlled so that you can pray.

1 Peter 4:7

Create in me a pure heart, O God,
    and renew a steadfast spirit within me.
Do not cast me from your presence
    or take your Holy Spirit from me.
Restore to me the joy of your salvation
    and grant me a willing spirit, to sustain me.
Then I will teach transgressors your ways,
    and sinners will turn back to you.
Save me from bloodguilt, O God,
    the God who saves me,
    and my tongue will sing of your righteousness.
O Lord, open my lips,
    and my mouth will declare your praise.

Psalm 51:10–15

"Not by might nor by power, but by My Spirit," says the LORD of hosts.

Zechariah 4:6 NASB

Those who belong to Christ Jesus have crucified the sinful nature with its passions and desires.

Galatians 5:24

Then Jesus said to his disciples, "If anyone would come after me, he must deny himself and take up his cross and follow me."

Matthew 16:24

Flee immorality. Every other sin that a man commits is outside the body, but the immoral man sins against his own body.

1 Corinthians 6:18 NASB

But immorality or any impurity or greed must not even be named among you, as is proper among saints.

Ephesians 5:3 NASB

For this is the will of God, your sanctification; that is, that you abstain from sexual immorality.

1 Thessalonians 4:3 NASB

Now the deeds of the flesh are evident, which are: immorality, impurity, sensuality.

Galatians 5:19 NASB

Your Spiritual Entourage

Friends Making Fun of You

Consider it pure joy, my brothers, whenever you face trials of many kinds.

James 1:2

But I say to you, love your enemies and pray for those who persecute you.

Matthew 5:44 NASB

Never pay back evil for evil to anyone. Respect what is right in the sight of all men.

Romans 12:17 NASB

For I consider that the sufferings of this present time are not worthy to be compared with the glory that is to be revealed to us.

Romans 8:18 NASB

Wanting God's Forgiveness

In Him we have redemption through His blood, the forgiveness of our trespasses, according to the riches of His grace.

Ephesians 1:7 NASB

Therefore let it be known to you, brethren, that through Him forgiveness of sins is proclaimed to you.

Acts 13:38 NASB

Therefore there is now no condemnation for those who are in Christ Jesus.

Romans 8:1 NASB

If you confess with your mouth Jesus as Lord, and believe in your heart that God raised Him from the dead, you will be saved.

Romans 10:9 NASB

He Himself bore our sins in His body on the cross, so that we might die to sin and live to righteousness; for by His wounds you were healed.

1 Peter 2:24 NASB

When you were dead in your transgressions and the uncircumcision of your flesh, He made you alive together with Him, having forgiven us all our transgressions.

Colossians 2:13 NASB

Forgiving the Girl

If you forgive men when they sin against you, your heavenly Father will also forgive you.

Matthew 6:14

My heavenly Father will also do the same to you, if each of you does not forgive his brother from your heart.

Matthew 18:35 NASB

Whenever you stand praying, forgive, if you have anything against anyone, so that your Father who is in heaven will also forgive you your transgressions.

Mark 11:25 NASB

Feeling Guilty

By grace you have been saved through faith; and that
not of yourselves, it is the gift of God.

Ephesians 2:8 NASB

Let us then approach the throne of grace with confi-
dence, so that we may receive mercy and find grace
to help us in our time of need.

Hebrews 4:16

For what I am doing, I do not understand; for I am not
practicing what I would like to do, but I am doing the
very thing I hate. But if I do the very thing I do not want
to do, I agree with the Law, confessing that the Law is
good. So now, no longer am I the one doing it, but sin
which dwells in me.

Romans 7:15–17 NASB

Your Spiritual Entourage

149

Fighting the Memory

Do not be anxious about anything, but in everything, by prayer and petition, with thanksgiving, present your requests to God. And the peace of God, which transcends all understanding, will guard your hearts and your minds in Christ Jesus. Finally, brothers, whatever is true, whatever is noble, whatever is right, whatever is pure, whatever is lovely, whatever is admirable—if anything is excellent or praiseworthy—think about such things.

Philippians 4:6–8

I consider that our present sufferings are not worth comparing with the glory that will be revealed in us.

Romans 8:18

And the God of all grace, who called you to his eternal glory in Christ, after you have suffered a little while, will himself restore you and make you strong, firm and steadfast.

1 Peter 5:10

Notes

Sign #3: Mr. Needy

1. *Seventeen* News, "National Survey Conducted by *Seventeen* Finds That More Than Half of Teens Ages 15–19 Have Engaged in Oral Sex," news release, Feb. 28, 2000.

2. Meg Meeker, M.D., *Epidemic: How Teen Sex Is Killing Our Kids* (Washington, DC: LifeLine Press, 2002), 16.

3. Megan Rauscher, "Oral Human Papillomavirus (HVP) Is Tied to Sexual Behavior and HIV Status," HIVandHepatitus.com, March 10, 2004, http://www.hivandhepatitis.com/recent/ois/humanpapillomavirus/031004l.html.

Sign #7: The Great Depression

1. Kara Joyner and J. Richard Udry, "You Don't Bring Me Anything But Down: Adolescent Romance and Depression," *Journal of Health and Social Behavior* 41 (2000): 369–91.

2. Armand M. Nocholi Jr., M.D., ed., *The Harvard Guide to Psychiatry*, 3rd ed. (Cambridge, MA: Belknap Press, 1999), 622–23.

3. A. M. Culp, M. M. Clyman, and R. E. Culp, "Adolescent Depressed Mood, Reports of Suicide Attempts, and Asking for Help," *Adolescence* 30 (1995): 827–37.

4. Meeker, *Epidemic*, 63.

5. "Third Annual Teen Sex Survey," *Teen People*, October 2005, http://www.prnewswire.com/cgi-bin/stories.pl?ACCT=104&STORY=/www/story/09-01-2005/0004098609&EDATE=.

6. Lydia A. Shrier, Sion Kim Harris, and William R. Beardslee, "Temporal Associations Between Depressive Symptoms and Self-reported Sexually Transmitted Disease Among Adolescents," *Archives of Pediatrics and Adolescent Medicine* 156 (2002): 599–606.

Sign #8: No U-turns

1. Walter A. Elwell and Philip Wesley Comfort, *Tyndale Bible Dictionary*, Tyndale Reference Library (Wheaton: Tyndale, 2001), 550.
2. Merriam-Webster's Collegiate Dictionary, 10th ed., s.v. "Repent."

Michael DiMarco is the CEO of Hungry Planet, a company that creates cutting-edge books to connect with the multitasking mind-set. Michael has also held positions as a chief marketing and creative strategist for Teen Mania, a university women's volleyball coach, a morning show DJ, and the host of a humor/advice radio program called *Babble of the Sexes*. Michael has co-written a number of books on relationships including *Marriable*, *The Art of Rejection*, *The Art of the First Date*, and most recently the teen dating book *B4UD8* with his wife, Hayley.

Hayley DiMarco is chief creative officer and founder of Hungry Planet, where she writes, co-writes, or edits all of the company's content for teens and former teens. She has written or co-written numerous bestselling and award-winning books, including *Dateable*, *Mean Girls*, *Sexy Girls*, *Technical Virgin*, and *B4UD8*. Michael and Hayley live in Nashville, Tennessee, with their daughter.

"Feeding the World's Appetite for Truth"

What makes Hungry Planet books different?

Every Hungry Planet book attacks the senses of the reader with a postmodern mind-set (both visually and mentally) in a way unlike most books in the marketplace. Attention to every detail from physical appearance (book size, titling, cover, and interior design) to message (content and author's voice) helps Hungry Planet books connect with the more "visual" reader in ways that ordinary books can't.

   With writing and packaging content for the young adult and "hip adult" markets, Hungry Planet books combine cutting-edge design with felt-need topics, all the while injecting a much-needed spiritual voice.

Why are publishers so eager to work with Hungry Planet?

Because of the innovative success and profitable track record of HP projects from the best-selling *Dateable* and *Mean Girls* to the Gold Medallion-nominated *The Dirt on Sex* (part of HP's The Dirt series). Publishers also take notice of HP founder Hayley (Morgan) DiMarco's past success in creating big ideas like the "Biblezine" concept while she was brand manager for Thomas Nelson Publishers' teen book division.

How does Hungry Planet come up with such big ideas?

Hayley and HP general manager/husband Michael DiMarco tend to create their best ideas at mealtime, which in the DiMarco household is around five times a day. Once the big idea and scope of the topic are established, the couple decides either to write the content themselves or find an up-and-coming author with a passion for the topic. HP then partners with a publisher to create the book.

How do I find out more about Hungry Planet?

Use the Web, silly—www.hungryplanet.net

Dating or waiting?
First date or 500ᵗʰ?

B4UD8

7 THINGS
YOU NEED TO KNOW
BEFORE
YOUR NEXT DATE

HAYLEY & MICHAEL DiMARCO

Hungry Planet tells you everything you need to know.

Available wherever books are sold.

If what you're showing ain't on the menu, keep it covered up!

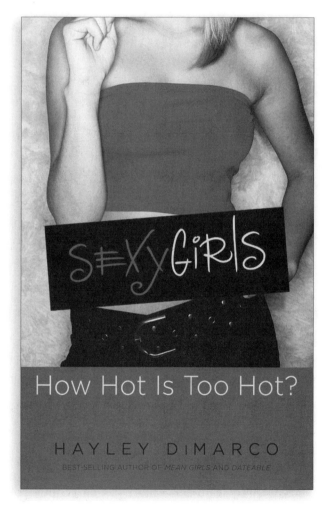

SEXY GIRLS

How Hot Is Too Hot?

HAYLEY DiMARCO

BEST-SELLING AUTHOR OF *MEAN GIRLS* AND *DATEABLE*

Available wherever books are sold.

what is **TECHNICALLY** *pure?*

Available wherever books are sold.

Revell
a division of Baker Publishing Group
www.RevellBooks.com

Hungry Planet
www.hungryplanet.net

‹iFuse›
life + faith + love + truth

life + faith + love + truth

Hayley DiMarco's Page

Hayley DiMarco
Female
Nashville, TN, United States
+ Add as friend
⊠ Send a Message
⋕ Share

Latest Activity

Hayley DiMarco left a comment for Brittany
1 day ago

Erin left a comment for Hayley DiMarco
1 day ago

Taylor and Hayley DiMarco are now friends

1 day ago

Hayley DiMarco added the blog post 'Sexy Fashion Fixes'
1 day ago

Hayley DiMarco left a comment for Erin
1 day ago

Hayley DiMarco left a comment for Katie
1 day ago

Hayley DiMarco is chief creative officer and founder of Hungry Planet, where she writes and creates cutting-edge books that connect with the multitasking mind-set. She has written and co-written numerous bestselling books for both teens and adults, including *Dateable*, *Mean Girls*, *Sexy Girls*, and *Technical Virgin*. She and her husband, Michael, live in Nashville, Tennessee.